Allegany Hellbender Tales

To Mom, a very good scout

Allegany Hellbender Tales

Larry Beahan

Coyote Publishing of WNY
5 Darwin Drive
Snyder, NY 14226
larry_beahan@adelphia.net

2003

ISBN 0-9703104-1-2

On the cover of this book is an Allegany Hellbender, the largest species of Salamander in the United States, up to twenty-nine inches long. They thrive in swift clean water and have lost much of their habitat. This photo is from the Buffalo Museum of Science's collection, taken in the 1930's at its famous "School in the Forest"
in
Allegany State Park.

On the back cover there is a photo of Alex and Angie, two of my grand children. We were canoe-camping on Kinzua Reservoir. Maybe someday they will see a Hellbender
in
Allegany State Park.

Larry Beahan 2002

Contents

Acknowledgements

My thanks to New York State, its Governor, George Pataki, his Office of Parks and Historic Preservation, Ed Rutkowski, George Wyman, Mike Miecznikowski, and OPRHP Commissioner, Bernadette Castro. As this book will show, that does not mean that I have agreed with all their Park Management decisions. But I must lay deserving credit where it belongs. In my seventy years of enjoying Allegany State Park, they and their predecessors have kept Allegany a marvelous, hilly green forest with living space for all kinds of plants and creatures including 350-year-old hemlocks, bear, deer and people It is the best Park in the world.

My mother, Dorothy Beahan, led our family's interest in this natural paradise near-to-home. She made her first visit to the Park at 18 in 1924 and her last at 90 in 1996. She first brought me down to the Park in 1932 when I was 2. I dedicate this book to her.

I need to thank the Allegany State Park Historian, the Salamanca Republican, Adirondack Magazine, and the Buffalo News for the encouragement they gave me by publishing my writings about the Park in their pages.

I do, particularly, need to thank Bob Schmid and the Buffalo Museum of Science for the photos they loaned me to use in this book.

Finally, I am indebted to: the Allegany State Park Historical Society, Friends of Allegany, the Adirondack Mountain Club, Sierra Club, the Summit Fire Tower Restoration Committee, the Allegany Deer Management Unit and I am also indebted to their individual members. They have given me hours of pleasure and companionship hiking, talking, planning and working in the Park. I would cite all those people I have in mind by name, but that would fill the entire book and I need some space for my stuff.

I'll just name one, Lyn, my wife. I thank her for her tireless editing and her unbounded support.

Introduction

This is a deeply personal book of my encounters with, the best park in the world, Allegany State Park. My family and I have used the Park for a long time. Mom and Dad came down here as newlyweds. They brought my sister, Marj and me for week-long summer vacations on Gypsy, Ryan and Dowd Trails and sent us to Camp Bee Tee Vee. I was here as a Boy Scout. My wife, Lyn, and I were camp counselors one summer at Arrowhead. It was our honeymoon. We have had good times here with our kids and our grand kids. Two of them Alex and Angie, are on the back cover.

I was away from camping and hiking and Allegany for some years. I got back to it through the Adirondack Mountain Club and Sierra Club. They drew me back into enjoyment of the outdoors and concern for the preservation of such places as Allegany and its great aging forest. The Allegany State Park Historical Society put me in close touch with Park's land, its people and its origins.

Over the last ten years, 1993-2003, I have written my observations and opinions about the Park into the essays, articles and stories which are gathered here. They are in a chronological order approximating that of their writing. They are accounts of Park experiences heard from many voices, some are history. A few are fiction. And there are issues. I hope that these Allegany Hellbender Tales will entertain and inform you readers and that you all get as much fun out of the Park as I have.

Medicine Man
at
Sinking Swamp

We would-be nature writers sat in a row at the edge of the pond while his bog-soft voice enveloped us. The afternoon sun yellowed the green trees and brush that were just starting into orange, yellow and red all around us. Geese on the pond retreated silently into the sky at our approach, then drifted back to squabble on the water, self-consciously, as if they did not want to interrupt him.

He was a big man in the Indian way, big chest, big stomach, hair long and black, kind of like a bear. His tee-shirt, cargo-pocketed shorts and approachable manner made him more of a Smoky Bear. "The animals," he said follow the Great Spirit's original instructions. They do things sensibly. It's people who don't follow instructions. Walk into any supermarket. Why package milk in so many different containers and make waste and pollution. Why not use glass and wash and refill it.

He made more sense in what he had to say about man and nature then anyone I had heard in a long time. There was some of it that didn't make sense, too, but even then he was fascinating.

He gave us each a pinch of tobacco to start with and then he lit his pipe and carried it around to each of us so that the smoke would purify us, or so he said. Anyway it set a fine mood. He had a plastic bag of sagebrush leaves and crushed a little for the wonderful odor. He gave us each a sprig of the dried gray-green aromatic plant to take home. "Smudge a little of it when you want to start writing something," he told us. "It'll help get you started."

And it did.

Red house Administration Building

Description of the Park

(From the Adirondack Mountain Club's *Wilderness Weekends in Western New York*, edited by Wilma and Frank Cippola.)

This 100-square-mile New York State park, directly north of Allegany National Forest, is the largest in the New York State Park System. Its 90-year-old mostly mixed-hardwood forest has, imbedded in it, stands of 350-year-old hemlock. The Park's lumber resources and subsurface oil and gas deposits have been the center of longstanding controversy. The Park's terrain is steeply contoured with ridges sloping into scenic valleys. It is especially beautiful in the fall when maples turn it crimson. The Park is the traditional hunting ground of the Senecas and still yields a harvest of fish, deer and bear.

Red House Lake before any Park buildings

The Seneca Nation's Allegany Reservation surrounds most of the Park as it follows the curve of the Allegany River. The

Seneca Museum in Salamanca is a source of local lore as is the Park's own "Larkin Store" museum at Quaker Run.

Larkin Store Museum

Allegany State Park is divided into Red House in the north and Quaker Run in the south. Each section has a designated camping area, a share of the four-hundred rental cabins, a restaurant, a store and a large lake of its own with swimming and boat launching sites. Friends Boat Launch gives access to the Allegany Reservoir at Tunesassa (meaning fine gravel in Seneca), the site of the old Quaker Indian School (1798-1938). Administrative Headquarters are in the chateau-like building overlooking Red House Lake. Trail maps and schedules of naturalists interpretive programs and many other events are available there as well as at the Quaker Rental Building.

The Park has 53.5 miles of hiking trails, 27 miles of ski trails and, on a separate specialized map, 55 miles of trails designated for both horses and snowmobiles. Hikers may use all of these trails. There are 400 miles of abandoned railroad track and many unmarked pathways that can mislead hikers. It is easy to get lost. So take a map and compass for even short jaunts.

Park hiking trails are marked with blue metal discs bearing hikers. The North Country-Finger Lakes complex uses painted white blazes. Ski trails have orange discs with skiers. Snowmobile trails are indicated by images of their machines in white on red backgrounds, and horse trails by yellow discs with riders. The surest way for a hiker to get back to a Park road is to follow the blue discs.

There is a paved bicycle trail around Red House Lake.

Numbered ASP trails:

1. Tuscarora Fire Tower: Five miles one way from Coon Run along the ridge, past the fire tower to an overlook above the confluence of Quaker Run and the Allegany, thence to ASP 3 near the toll barrier. It has the steepest incline of any trail in the Park.

2. Bear Caves-Mount Seneca: Four miles one way between trailheads off ASP3 at the Diehl Campsite and the Kaiser Cabins. Save yourself a lot of anguish. Pick up a detailed trail description at a rental office. It is easy to miss entering the wonderful caves. It is also easy to get lost.

3. Black Snake Mountain: Three-mile loop named for a Seneca Chief. At ASP 3 it ascends moderately into woods as it follows the edge of a basin. It rewards with a magnificent view.

4. Three Sisters: A three-mile loop off ASP 3 traversing three small mountains. Rated "more rugged" by the Park. Look out for poison ivy.

5. Bear Springs: Steep half-mile one-way hike off ASP 1. The start is located 2.5 miles north of the Quaker Rental Office.

6. Beehunter: Maintained by the Adirondack Mountain Club, this six-and-a-half-mile almost-loop runs between trailheads one opposite the Red House beach and the other in the Beehunter Cabin area. It is steep in places as it traverses ridges and valleys. Its south end approaches the National Fuel Gas natural gas storage field. Try a one way hike north by taking France Brook Road and the barred-to-vehicle-traffic road through the gas field. At the northern extremity of that road a short bushwhack intersects with Beehunter.

7. Osgood: A two-and-a-half-mile loop with trailhead on ASP 2 at the McIntosh Cabins Trail. It is a long, tough, uphill slug

from an elevation of 1420 to 2090 feet. It is often wet but rewards with curious huge rocks and magnificent views.

8. Red Jacket: Named for famous Seneca Chief buried in Buffalo's Forest Lawn is a one-mile loop, self-guided nature trail. The trail is located immediately behind the Red House Administration Building. Borrow a guidebook there and find out about the hay-scented fern, find where the Belted Kingfisher lives, discover what a pelecypod is and learn where the gooseberries are kept.

9. Finger Lakes/ Conservation Trail (ASP section): The North Country Trail comes into the Park from the National Forest in Pennsylvania and links up with the Conservation section (maintained by the Foothills Trail Club) of the Finger Lakes Trail. It makes an 18 mile traverse of the Park as Trail 9. In its course it runs the Mt. Tuscarora Ridge, crosses Coon Run, then ASP 3 near the Kaiser cabins, goes up Stony Creek Valley, visits the Big Basin and exits northward at Bay State Road near the Red House toll booth. This route has three lean-tos for backpackers.

10. (ASP) Conservation Trail: This four-mile loop partially overlaps with the trail above. It begins behind the Red House Administration building and because of its complexity it's a good idea to stop inside for the detailed trail guide. The Park rates it as "rugged

11. Patterson Hiking and Ski-touring Trail: This three-and-a-third-mile section of the Art Roscoe Ski Area can be begun at the Summit Trailhead on ASP 1 or at the Bova Downhill Ski Area. It can be combined with trails 12, 13 and 14 to provide a 20-mile loop of skiing or hiking.

12. Ridge Run: This is a challenging seven-and-seven-tenths-mile ski trail, which begins at the Summit area. It can be done in a loop with Patterson or as an all-day trip past Thunder Rock to ASP 2.

13. Leonard Run Loop: Five and a half-mile ski into a remote eastern section of the Park. It loops off of and back on to Ridge Run.

14. Christian Hollow Loop: A three-and-half-mile ski-loop off Ridge Run with a connecting arm to Leonard Run. It has a vista overlooking the Allegany River valley.

15. Sweet Water Loop: A gentle three-and-eight-tenths-mile novice ski loop near the Summit Trailhead.

16: Flagg: Two miles one-way from Cain Hollow Campground to Quaker Beach. Beware of the poison ivy where the trail crosses open meadow.

17. Eastwood Meadows: A two-mile loop leaving the North Country Trail a half-mile from North Country's intersection with ASP 1. It is entirely flat, has a pleasant meadow overlook and crosses the Lonktow Hollow Snowmobile Trail. Don't let that big wide trail confuse you. Stick with the footpath and the blue metal discs.

18. Snow Snake Run: Named for the traditional Seneca winter game, it is a challenging four-and-nine-tenths-mile ski loop off Patterson. It is groomed for skating and classic striding. Beware of its long grades and sharp turns.

Mount Onondaga Tornado Blowdown Trail (.75 mi.) and Connector Trail (1.5 mi.)to the North Country Trail. The trailhead is located on ASP 1 about 2 miles north of the Quaker Rental Office. Watch for bears during berry season. Portions of this trail are steep. There is a brochure available that describes the tornado and the debatable salvage process.

Stone Tower Loop: Two-and-a-third-mile loop trail groomed for ski skating out of the west side of the Summit Trailhead.

DIRECTIONS: Take Rte. 219 S through Salamanca, then go W on Rte.17. Take exit 19 for Red House, 18 for Quaker Run.

FURTHER INFORMATION: CALL 716 354 9121 (Red House or 716 354 2182 (Quaker) for rental information, maps, schedules and hunting season dates.

U.S.G.S. maps: Limestone, Red House and Steamburg.

ALLEGANY
STATE PARK

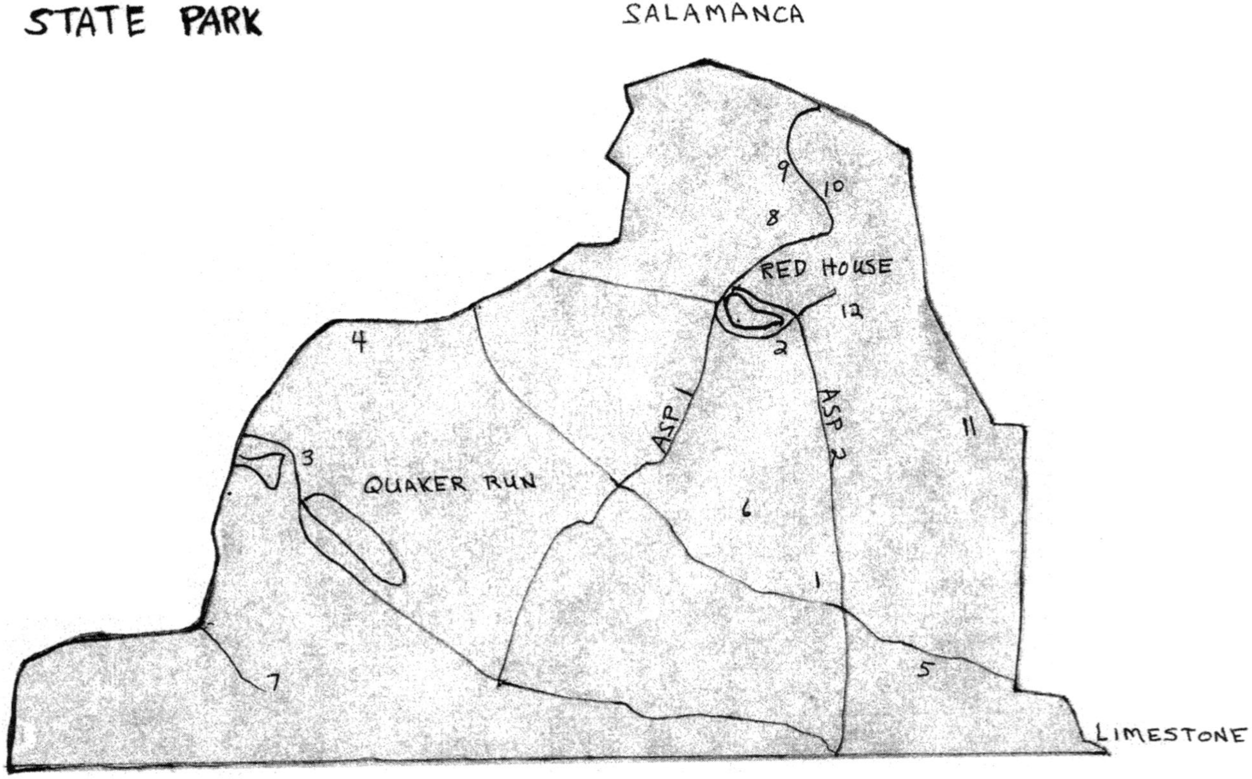

SALAMANCA

LIMESTONE

QUAKER RUN

ASP 1

ASP 2

RED HOUSE

1

2

3

4

5

6

7

8

9

10

11

12

Map Key

1. Camp 12
2. Dance Hall Site
3. Tunesassa, Friends Indian School
4. George Heron's Ga-hi-neh
5. Job Moses Monument
6. Gas Storage Field
7. Wolf Run
8. CCC Stone Tower
9. Abandoned Trail
10. Summit Firetower
11. New Ireland
12. Camp Allegany

Allegany Birthday Party

I am virtually sure of it, a black bear, a big black bear, took a picture of me. Look at the snapshot on the first page of this piece. Mom found it beside the cushion of my father's favorite chair. It is me. Mom says Dad took it in 1932. She says the shadow in the foreground is him sighting down through our old Kodak box camera.

Look at it. Does that shadow look like my father? Forgive me, you wouldn't know. That is not the shadow I would expect my father to make. To me, it is unmistakably the shadow of a large bear. See the ears and the sloping shoulders and the bulk of that body?

Some people believe you can tell more about a person by looking at his shadow than by looking directly at him. Vampires are said to cast no shadow at all.

It does not seem possible that I could remember anything from such an early age. Yet the moment Mom showed me this old picture I remembered the feeling of pleasure and awe. I can hear his deep baritone teasing me, "If you go down in the woods today, you're in for a big surprise. Today's the day the teddy bears have their picnic. Picnic time for teddy bears..."

I'm thinking, because talk did not, yet, come easily, ee-ya-- hoo, Daddy's home early from work. Hooray! Let's go see the bears, the other bears. Let's have a picnic in the park, too. He--y, hurry up, Daddy Bear, come pick me up.

Could it have been a coincidence that the day after Mom showed me this picture I had that amazing encounter with a black bear in Allegany State Park? I think not. It was no coincidence.

The next day, July 30, I attended the 75th anniversary of Allegany State Park. The gates of the Park opened in 1921. Mom started going there with girl friends in 1924. When Dad came down out of the Adirondack woods and they married in 1929, Mom showed him Allegany and he loved it. Our family has been going there ever since, to hike and picnic and camp and look for bears and raccoons and deer and salamanders and fungus. Dad used to love to find that dinner-plate fungus that smells so wonderfully of mold. The white ones with brown backs and he drew pictures on them, pictures of bears. Some of his pictures looked a lot like his shadow on that photo of us.

Quaker Rental Office way-back-when

So I went to the party that hot summer day. I've been worried about the Park. The lumber industry has been trying to persuade the State to let it harvest the ninety-year-old black cherry that grows there in abundance. National Fuel Gas owns a gas lease under the nine-thousand-acre stand of two-hundred-and-fifty-year-old hemlock. They want to cut it up with roads to re-bore old gas wells and make the dome at the center of the Park a vast natural gas storage tank. Bears and Pileated woodpeckers and eagles are not comfortable around a lot of roads, neither were me and Dad. We like deep woods to hide in.

Last year a general outcry came from the public. Assemblymen Sam Hoyt of Buffalo and Joe Pillittere of Niagara Falls articulated it well for us. If Dad were still alive he would have spoken up, too. I certainly did. At the last minute a promise came from Governor Pataki that he would not allow the commercial exploitation of our Allegany woods. Still, there are dangerous rumblings.

The day of the party it was storming. On the way to Allegany it gradually cleared. Then a glorious sun lit the green woods and hills and the speech made by the Commissioner of Parks. It was as if nature had magically colluded with the Parks Department and ordained a holiday truce for dear old Allegany's birthday. At the end of the day the torrential rain recommenced and this place so loaded with memories still seemed under threat.

The celebration centered about the museum that the Park authorities had made of the old Larkin Company Store. Its porch was draped in red, white and blue bunting. On the porch a bluegrass band blared out joyously. There was a flapper with shingled hair and a short slender dress like Mom used to wear. A sheriff's deputy dismounted and helped her onto his horse. Kids laughed as a pair of ponies pulled a cart full of them up and down the road.

Girl dressed as 1920's Flapper at 1996 Park Anniversary

In her speech Commissioner Castro skirted most of the important issues. She pointed to the commercial success of the Larkin Company Store in the Park. She made no mention of those loyal battlers Hoyt and Pillittere but she promised to name a part of the Park after a legislator who had not opposed logging and other commercial enterprises there. Ominously, she spoke of her hopes for the financial independence of the Park.

After the speech we all crowded inside to share a big chocolate cake decorated with a frosting map of the Park. People in shorts and tee shirts, officials in suits and dresses, costumed men in long black coats, women in big hats and bustles milled about stuffing themselves with cake as they congratulated one another on the success of the Park. My heart sank as the National Fuel Gas Corporate team laughingly dug an oversized chunk out of the heart of that map.

I got my cake and snuck out the back door to hike up to Dad's favorite spot, the three bear caves on Bear Cave Trail. On my way out I met my first bear of the day, a sweating girl pulling off a bear suit.

Koniag Eskimo women of Kodiak Island don bear skins while their men are hunting whales. They find that it helps the hunt. The Koniag also believe that people can become bears by eating bear meat. I suppose the opposite might also be true. Dad's dad used to go out after a bear once in a while, to carry them through the winter. Pickings were kind of thin up in the woods sometimes. Maybe that's how Dad got to be a bear.

Even under that dense canopy of maple and cherry, it was hot work climbing the trail to the caves. Sweating, I arrived at the long ridge of house-sized rocks where those three caves are supposed to be. I could not find the cave entrances. I am glad Dad didn't see that.

Fortunately, a man with his eleven-year old son and three other cave rats came up the trail. They offered me a flashlight and invited me along, after informing me that a ranger told them there were twenty-five bears in the Park. You can have your politicians and your speeches. Give me the woods and the bear caves. This is what I come to Allegany for.

Yet, there were moments when I started to question my dedication to the spelunking part of this expedition. The cave entrances are small. Inside they are dark and cool but some places are quite narrow. I would not like to surprise a bear there. One of the caves goes down and back more than thirty feet. I stuck it out, though, and explored all three caves almost as fully as the kids.

There were to be more speeches and I felt obliged to attend them. I thanked my companions and left them. I started the drive back to the Larkin Store following a Park police cruiser.

A big black bear, definitely not a girl in a bear suit, strode across the road in front of the cruiser. The cop got on his radio and was he animated.

I pulled over to watch. So did the bear. He lumbered twenty feet into the brush and turned his tan snout and big black ears and brown eyes to take us in. Then he went up on his hind legs for a better look. He was enormous, those great big paws and the teeth. It was him. I'll swear it was him. He gave me a grin that I know well, just like when he got off work early and had something planned for us. He knew about that birthday cake. He was teasing me. He was saying, "Save me a hunk of that birthday cake, will you, son?"

I did not get a good look at his shadow. He was laying on top of it. Anyway, I told him "Pop, we're going to do you better than a piece of cake. We're going to save these whole woods for you."

Then he was gone.

Buffalo Turn Verein and Arrowhead Group Camp 12

BEE TEE VEE

A big black furry bear came lumbering down the path passed the mess hall and toward the long green dormitory cabin where my cousin Art and I had pulled our cots together so as not to be so lonesome. That summer of 1938, Art and I were both eight and my sister, Marge, was six. It was the first time away from home more than overnight, for any of us. Of course I had never seen a bear close up like that so I started down the road right after him. He was too shy to let me pet him, fortunately.

From 1931 to 1942 the Buffalo Turn Verein ran a summer camp near France Brook Road just off ASP 2. The Turn Verein was a German-style YMCA (The main headquarters on High Street in Buffalo had a bar and one-armed bandits in addition to a pool and gymnasium) organized in Buffalo in 1853 as a branch of the international Turners. Friedrich Ludwig Jahn founded that organization in Germany in 1809 on the principals of "Frisch, From, Froelich und Frei" or Health, Faith, Joy and Freedom, more freely translated, "A Sound Mind in a Sound body."

Of course we didn't know any of that. We were just there to have fun in the woods. Mom and Dad had come down on the weekend to make sure we were set for the second half of our stay. We told them, or at least they told us that we told them, "Sure, we like it. It's OK." I, however, sent a secret message. I wrote in chalk inside of the suitcase in which we sent back our dirty laundry, "I want to come home." Marge was actually under the camp minimum age but the cook was Art's aunt and she promised to look out for her and us. On that first parents' day visit Mom brought a huge supply of graham crackers frosted with chocolate fudge, a new discovery for me. With that and a chance to make an acquaintance with a bear and generally getting used to the place, by the time Mom and Dad got my secret message, none of us wanted to leave.

One night, during our campfire out by the flagpole, my bear

joined us for a snack. Mister Andy Lascari, the camp director, looked so funny when my old bear tore the door off the garbage shed right in the middle of Andy's trying to teach us "Ich kan spielen auf der viola." I don't know what an Italian was doing trying to sing that kind of a song or what he was doing in such a "dutchie" setting anyway.

Bee Tee Vee Mess hall about 1939

But Andy was good. Art was a fussy eater. Once he wouldn't eat the canned pears his aunt had given us for dessert. Our table poppa called Andy over to discipline Art. Andy sat down on the bench beside my defiant cousin saying, "All right Arthur, since you won't eat your pear, your punishment is that for dessert you may only have half a pear." He took Art's spoon and carefully cut the pear in two. Then Art ate his half portion without complaint.

When our families came down on the weekend, Art's aunt roasted more turkey for them than they could possibly eat. The next week we had the most delicious turkey goulash with inch-and-a-half cubes of white meat floating in tomato sauce over succulent noodles. Art didn't even like that; tell you the truth, after a while I even got a little tired of it. The three of us came back to Camp Bee Tee Vee in 1939. The Park had added a spanking new recreation building alongside the mess hall where Andy had us woodcarving, working in leather and boondoggling. By then we were old timers. We knew the way to Thunder Rock, how to catch salamanders and at least Art and I had mastered the technique of catching water snakes in the rock-lined swimming pool and snapping their heads against rocks to them. For that service we were rewarded with a free trip to the camp candy shop.

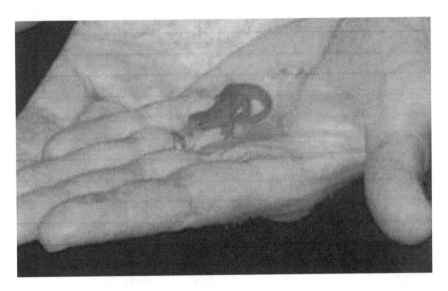

There was a huge rainstorm at the end of our two weeks. The creek flooded so we could not get across it to the athletic field, ASP 2 or the swimming pool. We didn't need the pool, we were having too much fun fooling around in the creek. Our folks had some trouble fighting their way through the flood. They were all too eager to rescue us back to civilization.

We had learned a lot but we remained curious for several years about what the older kids saw in those "midnight fungus hunts" they were always laughing about.

ARROWHEAD

In June 1953, Art was in the Navy in Guam, Marge was working with Quakers in Mexico and Lyn and I got married in Buffalo. We had no money, no place to stay, no jobs and I had two more years of medical school to do. So we took a two-month honeymoon back at Group Camp 12.

The Jewish War Veterans ran Camp Arrowhead there from 1946 to 1962. It seemed strange to have been there when it was such a German place, to have lived through World War Two with the Nazi persecution of the Jews and then to return there under a Jewish administration. Joe Manch, who later became the popular

Superintendent of Buffalo schools, directed the camp and as far as I could see he followed the same old Turnerian principles, only maybe in Yiddish instead of Hoch Deutsch.

Party at Arapaho, our Cabin, 1953

Joe had a manner about him that immediately commanded respect and attention even from thirteen year-olds. It was something about his ex-football player stance and steady gaze and what you knew he expected of you. He would stroll out in front of the kids on our assembly field and they would line up and fall silent without a command. When he wasn't there, I'd get out on the field and yell at them through a megaphone, promise to cancel their desserts and then sometimes they would quiet down when we started to hand out the mail.   My commanding demeanor improved under Joe's coaching.

The old rock pool had been replaced by a cement one, the two great halls had been joined into one, cabins had been refurbished and rearranged, there were showers and much better outhouses.

Joe put Lyn in charge of a cabin full of little girls, some younger than Marge was. Lyn worked harder than I did even though I was Assistant Head Counselor, Evening Program Director, Camp Doctor, Waterfront Director and had a cabin full of the bigger boys. Joe could have added Catholic Chaplain to our titles because Lyn and I were hired partly on the basis that we were Catholic and that we would take the two Catholic kids in camp to church on Sunday.

Camp 12 Arapaho 2002

One weekend, Joe and his Head Counselor left me in charge. That added Acting Director, Head Counselor and Jewish Chaplain to my titles.   On Saturday morning I wound up conducting Jewish services wearing a yarmulke and leading the few holy Jewish songs that I had learned that summer.

As I conducted that service, Andy Lascari's Italian-sounding last name did not seem so out of place from back in the Turn Verein days.   We Irish, Italians, Jews, and Germans all seemed to be looking for about the same thing in those delectable, cool, wooded hills between Quaker Run and Red House Creek.

One-Room School House

Bay State School, Red House 1890

Hook France, former Park Ranger, life-time Park resident and Master of Ceremonies, led off this story-telling marathon on one-room Allegany-State-Park school days. "Andy lived next door to the school. His job was to build a fire in the stove for us, every morning. But he never started till fifteen minutes before we got there. So we'd be cold and we'd be huddling around the fire. Leonard and Wesley got into a fight one morning. Leonard took off a boot and threw it at Wesley. He missed and it went through the window. The wind blew in there and it was <u>freezing</u> cold."

Once, I asked Hook, "How did people happen to call you Hook?"

He said "I don't know. Just, when we were kids, they started calling me that." Llewellyen is his real name and it comes to me that in dealing with Leonard and Wesley, Hook might have been a more effective moniker than Llewellyen. Roland "Rollie" Remington must have been really tough, surviving with that name.

Bay State School 1937

Hook, Roland, Jim Carr, George Heron and Charles Lindberg have borne up well under the physical wear and tear that goes with living into eight decades. But it was a stretch for our Park audience to picture these aging gents, in front of us, as grammar school kids. A stretch, till they got into their stories about when they attended one-room school houses in Allegany State Park or on the Seneca Allegany Reservation. Wisecracks and grins, twinkle of both voice and eye turned them into country boys firing spitballs, stoking wood fires and trudging through snow in the process of absorbing the "Three Rs."

I'm in their age range. If my family had lived in the vicinity of Allegany State Park I would have gone to one of those one-room school houses, too. I didn't. I went to kindergarten at the Academy School in suburban Williamsville and to Blessed Trinity grammar school in the heart of Buffalo. As I listened, I measured their experience against mine. I jotted down some notes and here's what I came up with:

To give us a general picture, Hook France listed the schools that were actually in the Park or on land that became Park. "There were two at Bay State and three at Red House, one lower down, one by the lake and one near Camp #10. There was France Brook,

Sunfish and Summit. The kids at one school knew nothing about any of the others. The schools were one room with one teacher and 7 to 20 students from first to eighth grade.

"I was at Bay State. One time the two teachers decided to give us a treat, a joint Christmas program with the Lower Red House School and Bay State. We went up there. Us kids were afraid, never been so far from home. It was like the other side of the world to us. Our teacher, Billy France, lined us up in chairs against the blackboard. The other kids were at their desks. We started hearing this clacking noise." Here Hook pantomimed ducking and looking over his shoulder. "Those kids were cutting up lead soldiers, winging them at us and hitting the blackboard."

Meanwhile, the Kindergarten Christmas Play in the Academy School in Williamsville in 1935 was held in a nice big warm auditorium. I was cast as the Toy Maker. All I had to do was go on stage, unlock the toy-shop door to start the play and get off the stage. I couldn't find the way off stage. That got a big laugh.

We moved to Buffalo in the middle of the school year. My first day at Blessed Trinity, Tom Keyes and some other guy beat me up. The second day, Jack Mc Mullen and I took care of them. Tommie and I were good buddies after that.

Burly, gray-headed Jim Carr stood up to speak. "In September 1933 I started at the upper Red House School. We had 8-15 students. The Park had started up then so we had Park employees' kids in school, too. We played a lot of baseball."

Hook interrupted Jim, "Bay State played Lower Red House in a soft ball game over by the stone pillars. I was the littlest guy so I was catcher. Big Jim comes running into home plate and knocked me clear into the pillars."

Jim held up a minute while the audience hooted, then went on with. "Remember we had a joint graduation of all the schools together. Had to buy a tie and a white shirt.

"Miss Kelly, Judge Kelly's sister, was our teacher. She went off to Europe for a year to work for the U.S. government.

"When I was in first grade our school, down below the dam, burned. Funny it was the night before school was going to start. They set us up in the Administration Building. Had to cut the Ranger Station in half for the next year to fit us in there. Then they rebuilt the school. The County Health Department would come in every year to give us a hearing test."

Larry and Marj

At Blessed Trinity we never had a fire but we certainly enjoyed it when Sister Remigia would clang her big brass bell in the middle of a school day and we would escape outdoors for a county-mandated fire drill. Baseball and fighting were our sports. I was a rotten pitcher and could neither catch nor hit a ball very well. So I did the best I could at fighting, though my glasses often got in the way.

Then it was Charles Lindberg's turn. "I came in after the school burned down. Our family had one of the Park houses up behind the Ad Building. My Dad was Chief Ranger. It was his office in the Administration Building that was used for the school. I hung around the Ad building a lot. I'd tell my Mom I was going to visit Mark and Lillian Smith's house and I'd go down to the school instead. I was done with first grade before my mother even knew I went to school.

"Our teacher, Loretta Kelly, went on a trip to Mexico. She came back with a whole shelf full of pottery. It was a miracle back then that anyone left Salamanca and went someplace.

"Friday afternoons we had our 'Movie Project.' The one I remember was actually a slide program---on Pompeii---little thing like that stays etched in your mind. And Friday afternoon was arts and crafts day. We did finger painting. Don Mendel, the Park Plumber's son, yelled out, 'If you see a fly with a blue ass he's been over here.'

At Blessed Trinity all our teachers were nuns. I never knew of any of them going anywhere except once in a while home to visit their folks. The convent, located behind the school playground, had wooden floors painted gray. There were no rugs or curtains. We didn't know whether our nuns, Sister Nolaska, Sister Mildred, Sister Remiga had more than one name or if the name they had was their first or their last name. Our big treat was going to communion on first Friday and having free breakfast in the school basement, milk and stale fry cakes donated by the Elite Bakery across the street. Once we got Dick Fisher laughing so hard he blew milk and fry cake out his nose.

Lindberg went on, "We had games we played. Musical Chairs and London Bridges. I don't care much for London Bridges. But we liked Musical Chairs. We were playing once and smoke started coming from Jim Carr's pants. He had a packet of them kitchen matches in his back pocket. Fortunately we had a crock filled with drinking water handy to put it out. The crock was always full. But you had to hope nobody spit in it.

Hook interjected. "Oh yeah, two of us were picked, for a month, to bring in a pail of water and fill up the crock everyday.

"We had a Miss Kelly too, Magdalena Kelly. She was bad. Red France's head should be flat, the way she'd pound his head with that fourteen inch ruler. Every morning, he'd set her off."

At Blessed Trinity our principal, Sister Mildred, was a skinny little woman but she had this three-corned ruler and she'd make you hold out your hand and whack you. Charlie Murphy was the worst and toughest kid in our class. He was short, fast and strong and so tough that he had two nick names Murky and Mango. Once, Sister Mildred ordered me to take him home to his mother. I remember thinking, "Sister, you got to be out of your mind."

George Heron, the oldest of our story telling students and former President of the Seneca Nation, took the floor. He talked in an even-paced way that seemed always to suppress a chuckle or a tear, "I went to the Indian School in Red House. My mother was a teacher. Then I went to Salamanca High School--- with Magdalena Kelly." And the audience laughed.

"There were seven district schools on the Reservation starting with Horseshoe up at the bend of the Allegany River and going down to Onoville, each four mile apart so no one had to walk more than two mile. I went to number three in Red House.

"I started in 1926. Our teacher was Georgia Carr. She was a kind woman. Every Friday she brought two quarts of milk--- crackers and sugar for a snack for us.

George Heron, 2002

"We had some man-sized boys, grown men, fifteen and sixteen, six foot--- in sixth grade. Our schools were spread out. Sometimes you had to walk two miles on a dirt road and in the snow. We didn't have anything like snowplows in them days."

In 1942, the really toughest and biggest kid in our sixth grade, Big Joseph, got drafted into the army.

Our streets were not plowed well and the big kick was to grab the rear bumper of a car and slide behind him, on the packed snow, as far as you could. I don't know how so many of us survived.

George said, "My mother went to Geneseo Normal School. She taught out west for five years, then she came back here. They sent her way back in the wilderness over to Onoville to teach. Them days we had the Doodle Bug running on the Pennsy track, one car with a motor, seats and baggage. My mother got on at Red House and rode it as far as Wolf Run. There was an old man named George. He'd pole her across the river in a John boat. John boat had a flat front, flat back and bottom and no keel. In the winter there'd be big chunks of ice floating down the river. Then she had to walk another half mile.

Only nine students, so that school closed after two or three years."
George held up a picture of one of his mother's classes from Old
Town. "They're mostly long gone," he said.

Seneca Reservation School

*In Buffalo we had about a half mile to walk to school. It was a
sociable time, walking and talking with other kids except in
snowball season. Then it was war all the way and the baseball
players were mean about it.*

Changing pace, George went on recalling teachers. "Mister
Mann and Georgia Carr--- they were the difference between
heaven and hell." The audience laughed. "Mister Mann, he'd cuff
up his own boy even more than anyone else.

"Emma Wolf was the school Superintendent. Old maid they
called her then. She was a big strong woman. Had to be to stand up
to them Indian women." His voice rose in mock female ire, 'You
put my boy in that sand box. How you know people don't spit in
there?'

"Stanley Johnson was school principal. He got up a harmonica
band and they had a radio show going. Wayne Printup was in it."

Wayne waved from the audience. "Kids made tom-toms and such to sell. Don't know what happened to the money. Guess it went in Johnson's pocket. They made up that patriotic song, 'Liberty Man' and got it published.

"We had to cross the Allegany on a bridge on the way to school. We'd grab a big rock and watch for a school of carp. When there was a bunch, we'd drop them. Once in a while we'd see a fish turn over. We got a big kick out of that. Don't know why.

"Most of the school houses were situated next to a cemetery.   Every funeral, the kids marched in line with the mourners. If it was a Civil War Vet the GAR fired their rifles. One vet's grandson came back from federal prison in Montana. He had iron manacles around his ankles. Then he had to go back. As little kids, at an early age, we learned what death was all about.

"In 1932 we got our first school bus. Called it the 'Cracker Box' because it looked that way, home made.

"When I started at Salamanca High School there were nine of us. By the time I graduated there were twenty. That's how fast education grew.

"In 1935 June La Croix and I graduated from Salamanca High School together." (June, long time a Red House Justice of the Peace, waved from the audience). "High School was the first time someone other than a Seneca sat in front of me or alongside of me. Pretty little blond girl smiled at me. I smiled back. I said, Heck these white people not such a bad lot after all."

At Blessed Trinity, we were all Irish, German and Italian Catholic. The only Indians we knew were in the Saturday afternoon matinees at the Central Park Theater. Toward the end of High School in 1948, a black girl joined us at Bennett High.

Rollie started in, "In 1938 I moved into the valley." He held up a picture. "This was the school house. It had a water pump inside this little addition and two backhouses behind. Morris Cavanaugh smoked cigarettes out there and I'd always bum one off him. We'd throw the butts down in there. The teacher never knew a thing about it."

"Oh yeah," called some former teacher from the back of the room and the audience got a laugh out of that.

"Our teacher never hit anyone," Rollie said. "All the bad kids were over on the Red House side."

"And you were all angels!" some former Red House student called back.

Roland said, "I might as well get this over before someone else brings it up. I never heard about the school on the Red House side burning down, but the one at Elko on the Quaker side did. I'm still wondering just how it happened but here's what I remember:

"They gave my father the job of school janitor. He couldn't do it, of course. He was running his own farm and a neighbor's, too. So I got the job and he gave me the whole $5-a-month pay. We got up a 4 AM to take care of our own dairy and after that the neighbor's. At 8 AM I'd go to the school and build the fire. And at night I went back over to fill the stove with wood so the fire would hold overnight. Weekends, I cut up pine stumps left from the old original lumbering. It made fine kindling.

"By seven PM, the night of the fire, I was so tired. I checked the fire in the stove but I didn't latch the stove door. Next morning I came up the road to get it going. I wondered who could be in our play yard with a lantern. There was a light going up and down. Then I realized the school was on fire. I slapped the flames with my gloves, and then ran for help. The school didn't burn down completely. One semester I went to the Indian school and after that to Randolph. That Elko School finally closed in 1946."

I remember a great weekend at the Park in 1946. The Boy Scout Explorer Post that I belonged to spent it in a cabin, owned by the parents of two of our members. It was on the Park Road along Red House Creek beneath the dam. The memorable thing about it was that by then we were advanced enough to bring dates. But back to Roland in grammar school.

Rollie said, "Harry France was a school trustee. The money to run the schools was raised in the local school district. Bob Banks was a trustee and paid all the bills, even though he lived in

Florida. Jenny Cargill was truant officer. She never had to chase anyone.

"One day they decided to let us have fun. They took us three quarters of the way around the world up to the playground in the Park We played baseball and had races. It was like getting on a plane and flying to Russia."

Holding up an old school photo, Rollie named off some of the kids. Then he came to one, "This girl on the left side, Florence, she was my girlfriend. Boy, she was a nice girl."

A classmate of Rollie's spoke up from the audience, "Remember in World War II we picked milkweed pods?"

Rollie answered, "Yes. I remember they were used in parachutes somehow. We'd put them in a plastic bag and hang them on a tree in the sun. We got 50 cents a bag."

A woman in the audience put up her hand and said, "My brother went to the Red House School. He listened in on a higher grade and skipped a grade. They took turns coming up to the teacher's desk, grade by grade, and then went back to their own desk to do their work assignment."

Rollie said, "You got individual attention."

She came back with, "That's how you got so smart. We were the best spellers and had the best handwriting."

Rollie stood, pointed a finger at the audience and said, "For the information of the younger people here, my father was in third grade when my grandfather was hit by lightning. So my father was taken out of school to run my grandfather's farm. He went to school some, but only when there was no work at the mill. At home we'd sit around nights and educate him."

Hook took over, "My father used to say when he went to school they had 39 kids in class. One more and they could have had two teachers.

"School ran from 8 till 12 and 12:30 to 4:30 with a half hour for lunch and a 15 minute recess in the morning and the afternoon. Baseball was our number one sport. I was the smallest, so I got right field and never came up to bat. Our library was a total of 50 books.

At Blessed Trinity we had 38 in my class for a while. The only hope of a smaller class was to go off to a dreaded "Public School." We had no library. Except that Sister Remigia had two shelves of books we could borrow. I read the whole 'Boy Allies in World War I' series. Of course just a few blocks away we had the Fairfield branch of the Buffalo Public Library system. I went through their young adults section and dug out all the frontier stories.

Master of Ceremonies, Hook France, took the floor to summarize. He said, "Of the Red House schools, Bay State was the oldest and the last to stand. It was built in 1851. My great grandmother went there. My grandmother, my dad and then me, last in line, all went to Bay State School. Ray Costello lived in it for a house. Park took it and didn't fix the leaking roof. Finally two years ago they bulldozed it and buried it in the ground."

Roland broke in, "There was a school on the Quaker side near Brow Trail, operated till June of 1942. Still there, cabin 11 on Barton Trail, near Coon Run."

Barton Trail Cabin Number11, 2002

34

Hook topped things off with, "My grandfather and a friend were the two biggest kids in school. The teacher would have them sit out in front on the stoop to do their studying and so they could spit. They were the only ones allowed to chew tobacco."

From the 1892 issue of:
"The History of Cattaraugus County, Chapter XLV, History of The Town of Red House:

It was not until 1851 that a school house was built in the town. And in it Caroline Barnes was the first teacher. This building was erected on the Little Red House creek.

In 1892 there were six school districts, in each of which a school was maintained; there were 211 scholars, who were under instruction of six teachers. The value of the school buildings and sites was $1,560, while the assessed valuation of the districts for school purposes aggregated $267,765. The amount of money received from the State was $768.89 and by local tax $ 184.20. The population of Red House in 1890 was 1156 against 487 in 1880.

A Trout in our Milk House

This is pretty much the way Roland Remington told it to me.

You know that clump of apple trees where you turn off the Quaker Road for Kane Hollow now? That's where the farm was that my Daddy moved us into in 1938.

City kids, who didn't know much about the country or fishing and things like that, used to come down and want to pet my pet fish. I remember Glen Schubert brought a friend down who got a pretty good surprise one time.

We didn't have any city water. Our water came from a spring right out of the hill. A pipe emptied it into a 55-gallon drum on our back porch. The overflow ran a hole in the ground in the milk house. All the farms used to have a building to keep the big ten-gallon cans of milk cold before they were picked up to go to the factory.

In 1939 or 40 we had the spring water piped into the house and on into the milk house. Dad built a concrete tank inside there, about 7 by 3 feet and 3 feet deep. We kept it filled up with cold spring water to put the milk cans into. Well, I used to catch trout out of the cricks and keep two or three of them in there for pets. I'd hunt night crawlers to feed them and the fish'd get pretty good sized.

I'd let kids come in and dangle a night crawler so the trout would leap up and grab it out of their fingers. But the kid Glen brought down, well he wasn't exactly a kid, he was twenty years old, and should of known better, well he teased the fish. He put a finger in the water and wiggled it around. Well you should have seen him leap. He got bit pretty bad. Went home with a bloody finger. You look at a trout careful; they got a pretty good little set of teeth.

The last pet trout I had got up to fifteen inches. When we moved out of the farm, Mom had me take him out of there carefully and put him back in the crick so's he'd live.

Bob Byledbal
The Impresario of Red House

"What did you do in the winter time?" someone in the audience asked Bob Byledbal during his August 1999 talk to the Allegany State Park Historical Society.

He laughed, "Nothing. I worked 16 hours a day from May through October running those Red House concessions. I went home and played in the basement with my model trains.

"Speaking of winter," Dave Remington piped in, "I have a belated confession to make. We local kids used to use your Red House dance hall for a roller rink in the winter time."

Bob waved that off with, "Oh, I knew that. I knew you wouldn't do no harm."

Someone came in with, "What about your wife, Thelma?"
That stopped Bob for a second, "Thelma wasn't my wife. She was my adopted summer wife, my second in command. Right after I started, Charlie Lapp, this big imposing guy in his Park Ranger uniform, came up to me and said, "You're going to hire my wife, aren't you?"

"Sometimes Thelma seemed to think it was her that wore the badge. Once she broke up a fight between two kids who had had a little too much beer. One kid was hiding under a car. Someone asked, 'What's he doing under there?' and was told. "He's afraid of Thelma."

"A guy came in the store and wanted Thelma to fill up his plastic container with white gas. We had an unbreakable rule against that, but this guy started an argument with Thelma. He came storming out the front, 'Officer, that woman in there insulted me.'
The Ranger he had accosted said, 'You mean my wife?'"

Bob Byledbal stood before 150 of us in the wood-paneled great room of the Tudor style Red House Administration building with its massive fireplaces and sweeping view of green mountains and blue lake. He could not have picked a more evocative setting to tell of his 21 years running the stores, hot dog stands, dances, dance halls and hi-jinks on the Red House side of Allegany State Park. No one tells tales of those halcyon days of the fifties, sixties and seventies better than this big, bald, laughing, moon-faced businessman turned stand-up-comic, purveyor of Park nostalgia. But the magic did not come from Bob alone. It sparkled back and forth between him and his audience of old Park employees, old and new Park visitors. One of his tales would kindle a recollection in someone else, which in turn would remind him of three more pungent or outrageous events and on and on.

Bob was born into this business. He worked for his parents who ran a store and dance hall on the Quaker Run side of the Park. At, as close as I can figure, 19 or 20 he took over running the concessions in Red House. Bob must have been a kid with maturity beyond his years when he started in this business. Now, in maturity, he easily turns kid again, telling of it.

He started this talk by recognizing old Park friends and employees, not a few of whom were present. Then he described the physical plant and the operation of an intense and complex business. Along the way he included the flukes, ironies and comic gyrations.

"The Red House store and dance hall were over by the bathhouse, where the miniature golf is now. The store was one of your plain square Allegany State Park buildings with the wooden rafters and open ceilings. It was hot, surrounded by blacktop, and got up to 101 degrees in there. We opened up a window at the side where you got your pop and ice cream."

"The dance hall was built on the solid concrete floor of what had been a dairy barn. The floor was bird's-eye maple and polished up beautifully. We used to get 1500 people in there at night. The floor in the Quaker dance hall would sag and the building would sway to the music under that load. The Red House floor wouldn't budge an inch. I had my own little apartment built on the back of it."

"I bought a marvelous charcoal grill from a place up on Transit Road. You fill that with red-hot charcoal and it got really hot. Put a steak on there, and in minutes it was charred on the outside and just pink on the inside. Cooked hot dogs and hamburgers really fast."

Miniature golf on the old dance hall and dairy barn floor

"Speed was the key to the business. Quick and clean. Mop three times a day; dust the cans every day. You'd come and order a hamburg, two hot dogs and three milk shakes and you'd have them in your hand hot and ready to go before you got done paying for them. Made them all up in advance and sold them as fast as they were done.

I trusted the kids with thousands of dollars. Steal even a bag of potato chips and you're out the door. Told the kids eat all you want, all the hot-dogs, hamburgs, milkshakes, you can hold. As long as you do it on break, on the premises, just don't take any home. Pretty soon they'd be showing up with their brown bag lunches. 'Ugh, can't stand another one of those hot dogs.'"

"The food was always fresh. If I wouldn't eat it, I wouldn't have it on the shelves. Nobody ever got sick."

"People worked with me, not for me. Each business had a manager that I consulted with every day. So there would be one boss on each job and I worked through him. I trained them. Some worked twelve hours a day, seven days a week to make a bundle of money for college. It was their choice. You could work a day or a week for me. I had an arrangement with Salamanca High for promising workers. Hired a lot of local kids and, after a while, the yearly kids, the ones whose families leased cabins by the year. They are doctors, lawyers, engineers, all over the country now and in Africa and China. They've gone on to good careers."

"But every year we had employee's day and they cut loose. The Park Police, the Rangers cooperated but made sure the kids put things right. A couple of cars wound up in the lake. One time they painted up an old outhouse and set it up for an entrance tollbooth. There was a statue everyone hated, up at the Administration Building, and it got cut up into shreds. We were accused of doing it but that wasn't us."

When Bob asked for questions, they came flying. "Bob, were you ever troubled by health inspectors?"

"Health inspectors, fire inspectors. The fire inspector came down and said, 'You have to keep those doors open or put a push bar on them.' So we kept them open."

"The health inspector came by, 'You've got to close those doors, the flies are getting in. I told the kids, 'When you see the fire inspector open the doors, when you see the health inspector close them.'"

"I had these good Szelengoski hamburgers all made up into patties that we used in the hot dog stand and I decided to package them up for sale in the store. Health inspector said, 'You can't do that. They have to be all labeled with what's in them and you can't put them back in the hot dog stand.' Can you believe it? They made me take kerosene and burn up 100 pounds of perfectly good hamburger."

"What about flies in the hamburger?" somebody called out.

"Yeah, well, it was in the country. In the country there are flies and mice and raccoons and squirrels and bats. One new girl was scooping vanilla ice cream. She asked me what to say about the flies. I told her, 'Tell them they're raisins.'"

"Nobody ever got sick."

"One of my managers filled a gun with bird shot and gave a dollar for every bat killed in the store."

Bob Schmid broke in with, "Kevin Berlson, you know he's the editor of the Salamanca Republican, now. He was telling me how when he worked in the store he took a 22 in there one night and he got so furious shooting at those pesky bats that he blew out half the lights."

"Bats were a problem. They closed one of the stores because of their droppings. They couldn't be controlled."

"Why'd you quit?" someone asked.

"Times changed. It was twenty years, time to move on. My wife and kids lived in Hamburg. I was tired of never being home on the Fourth of July, never taking the kids swimming. The State wanted to deal with just one vendor. Besides, there was the drug problem down here. Armed robbers chased me over the hill from Salamanca at 80 miles-an-hour. I got tired of sleeping with my shotgun."

Another question, "How about those Dawn Dances?"

"We had Dawn Dances and Caper dances. The place got so jammed, if there was a fight at the other end, I could never get there. Just had to let them fight. I had to move my disc jockey outfit into the apartment, no room. We'd start at 9 and dance till the sun came up. At the Caper Dances, in the middle of the evening we'd pull some kind of a stunt. A bunch of guys would walk in, yell, 'Finance Company,' and walk off with the cigarette machine. A bunch would carry in a kitchen table and chairs and sit down to play cards in the middle of the floor."

"I used to hang around the dances till about 2am, then go over and play cards with the Rangers working nights. This call came in that there was a drug party going on up on Kaiser Trail. They asked me to come along. One of the guys had this brand new Stetson hat of which he was very proud. We went over and surrounded the place in the dark and he snuck up to the porch rail. Just then a guy came out on the porch who had been drinking a lot of beer and he relieved himself right on the guy's new hat. And he couldn't say a thing."

Bob called out to Alonzo Sharp and Hook France, two retired Park Rangers, in the audience. "Sharpie and Hook, you knew I did all that, don't you?"

Roland Remington volunteered, "Me and another guy decided not to drink at a Dawn Dance, one of those nights. We picked up beer bottles instead and we completely filled up a 1936 Chevy. We made $125."

"Yeah, those Dawn Dances were close to being a Woodstock," Bob laughed contentedly. Now I've got a few pictures up here for you to look at. They aren't your ordinary scenery. They are just kids, sleeping, working, kissing. Then I want to take you all over to where the store was and I've got a couple more stories to tell."

Sorority Girls at Fancher Pool 1950

Allegany Moon

"Allegany moon keep shining, shining on the one who waits for me." These old lines came rolling out in a full baritone to engulf our silver-haired audience in waves of nostalgia. Thirty of us Allegany history buffs sat in the chapel just across the road from the Larkin Store museum in Quaker Run. We had gathered there to listen to former Allegany dance hall impresario, Bob Byledbal, talk about that unique experience of his in the 40's, 50's and 60's, the days of his and of our youth. But we had no idea he could still sing like that.

A chapel seemed at first the wrong place to reminisce about our early forays into picking up dates until Bob pointed out that the building was put together just the way the old dance halls were. We looked up at the exposed two-by-four rafters holding up the board ceiling and the continuous wrap-around-screened window with its elevatable shutters. Bob said, "There were plenty of times when a good wind would come up and knock out the supports so the shutters would all come down at once with a bang."

Bob is a tall, beefy guy, almost totally bald now. He was probably a good-looking teenager in the 50's when he started running dances. But who ever looks like that again? He smiled broadly during his presentation, obviously enjoying it as much as we were. He recalled, "We used to come down to the swimming area every Monday to check out which new sorority girls were in the Park. The guys made sure all the girls knew about the dances and that they would be very welcome."

I felt a little out of sync with all this. My visits to the two Allegany dance halls, one by Red House Lake and the other at the Quaker swimming pool, were mostly when I was younger. Or at least I felt younger. I did more watching and wishing than dancing.

Bob inherited his job from his father, who, with a partner, ran the dance hall concession beginning in 1951. Bob worked for his dad several years before he took over the business himself. He recalled that dancing was a tradition in the Park from its earliest times back in the 1930's. It was mostly square dancing to start with and it drew people from outside the Park as well as the Park campers.

Much of the time the music was provided by a jukebox. "You paid your admission and I fed quarters into the jukebox all night."

"What about the square dancing?" a woman called out from the back of the audience. "Leo Remington was my husband."

"Yes, Leo Remington called all the dances," Bob laughed.

"And everyone always wanted 'MacNamara's Band,'" she hollered back.

Bob started calling it, "First couple lead to the right, all hands round ..." you could almost hear the fiddle music and feel the floor begin to rock.

"Do you remember Enfield Strickland, the big tall guy who played the fiddle? He did all the arrangements," she called out.

Someone else said, "And Bob Remington's band played all the time."

Bob passed the ball back and forth easily with the audience. "Yeah, what was their name? The Mood Men. They were the Mood Men."

There was a tall, attractive couple sitting next to me in the audience reacting to each of the images that Bob called up for us. The woman was particularly striking. She fascinated me in that we had established the fact that we graduated from Bennett High School together. For the life of me I could not remember her. Nor could I figure out how she could look so good and be my age? The old left-out feeling crept up on me. She must have been one of the Bennett Queens that I looked at so longingly so long ago and with whom I never got to dance.

Bob went on, "Rock and Roll took over from square dancing. We had disc jockeys for a while. Then I thought, I can do that. So I took over the mike in 1959. Then in the 60's we moved on to garage bands, Salamanca garage bands, mostly two lead guitars and a drummer. The Continental Frets, the Jaguars, Baby Hughey and the Tiaras. The bands used to sleep in the back of the hall. We sold beer until a commissioner's son died in an unfortunate accident after a dance. We handed out Zippo lighters with Allegany emblems painted on them. They are worth a fortune now."

Bob took us from jitterbug through the twist. He handed out old 45-rpm records and let us stamp the backs of our hands with the authentic rubber stamp that he used back in the old days. Retired Park policeman Hook Franz held up his hand to verify that he worked nights at the dance hall to help keep order. Bob recalled the "Dawn Dances" that sometimes lasted all night and wound up with the band and all the dancers parading down and around the beach.

"Saturday night, we would always try to get into the square dances for the first set because...Do you remember what that was?" Then he started calling:

> Oh first you hug her
> Than you squeeze her
> Then you kiss her if you can.

"At the end of the week you always tried to wind up with a girl's telephone number and address. Nothing much ever came of it." Then he held up a clear plastic envelope about six inches square. "Here are two bottle caps from beers I shared with a girl and here is her address." The audience laughed and strained to look but he did not let us read what was written there.

"That was a long time ago. In the 70's, Disco came along and put us out of business. But lots of couples met at those dances, and married. The dances were the largest social events ever held in the Park. We could get a thousand people into the Red House hall. Over the years hundreds of thousands of people attended."

Bob closed with this announcement: "After we finish here we will go over to the old Quaker dance hall which is falling down and there we will have some music. You will have the privilege of the very last dance." Then he broke into a mellow:

> For it's a long, long time from May to December.
> But the days grow short when you reach September.
> When the autumn weather turns the leaves to flame,
> One doesn't have time for the waiting game.

A Park Full of Memories,
and
The Master Plan
1993

It knocked the wind out of me when I heard that they want to log Allegany State Park again. We won that fight in 1983 ten years ago. Now in 1993 Park officials have proposed another master plan that would log a quarter of the Park, at 500 acres a year.

Red House Saw Mill

Ziegfeld Girls

My family has been going down to Allegany since a skunk ran Mom and her "General Electric" girl friends out of their Buffalo Trail cabin in 1924. That was before Red House or the "new" administration building. I have a 1936 picture of Mom, Dad, me and my sister in our funny old woolen bathing suits. We are sitting on the concrete edge of the old Quaker Run swimming pool. Our folks sent my sister and me to the Turn Verein Camp on France Brook Road for a few summers. That was during "the war" when my mother went back to work. We hunted for little orange salamanders and big white fungus. Once, a full-grown black bear walked right through camp in broad daylight with me following him.

As a young fellow, my Dad was a lumberjack for a while in the Adirondacks. He never got the woods out of his blood. Allegany was the closest big woods around here and he got us there whenever he could. He showed me how to use an axe and build a fire and have a good time in the woods. We went back year after year and the woods kept getting bigger. That was the thing about Allegany; the trees there were big, like a real forest. Later I went there to meet girls at the old dance hall. I learned to canoe on Red

House Lake. The first big hill I ever skied was at the Bova Area. We used to wonder if anyone ever went off those ski jumps. I remember the power of the Allegany River when it flooded. One summer I took a girl for a picnic, climbing Thunder Rocks. We got married and spent our honeymoon as counselors in the Park. Those trees kept on getting bigger. We took our kids there to hike and camp and play.

Fancher Pool 1934

In 1921 the New York State Legislature enacted a law setting up Allegany State Park. It said the Park was to be, "forever reserved and maintained for the use of all the people" and "to provide for the protection and propagation of fish and game thereon and for the reforestation of the same." Now some of the people see those magnificent stands of cherry, ash and hemlock as board feet and money in the bank.

A million four hundred thousand people visit Allegany every year. Half of them are people from Buffalo, like us. We go there for a bit of peace and fun in a real woods with big trees. Let's get together and tell them to let the place alone. A friend of mine just got back from a week-end down there. She was excited. She had seen her first bald eagle. She didn't have to travel to Alaska.

Allegany is now a big enough, old enough forest to support those magnificent creatures, right here in Western New York.

Stony Brook beaver pond

We berate Brazil and Quebec for cutting down their old forests. We've cut down most of our own. We've got sixty-seven thousand acres of forest in Allegany that is now between 90 and 350 years old. Its unbroken canopy provides or is about to provide the rare habitat of a climax forest. Let's not sell this family treasure.

NYS Office of Parks and Historic Preservation Hearing on Allegany State Park Master Plan Buffalo 1993

Ivan Vamos Deputy Commissioner
NYS Office of Parks Recreation and Historic Preservation
Albany NY 12238

Mr. Vamos   March 16, 1993

I represent the 15,000 member Adirondack Mountain Club. Our Club has asked me to present two documents here at today's OPRHP hearing on the draft master plan for Allegany State Park.

The first document is an Adirondack Mountain Club resolution. Its main point is as follows; "We find that timber management in state parks in general and in Allegany State Park particularly, is incompatible with important recreational values and the primary mission of the Park." The resolution lists thirteen reasons for that opinion.

The second document is a legal brief prepared by the Counsel of the Adirondack Mountain Club. It reviews the relevant laws and concludes that there is no statutory authority for timber management or forestry activities in Allegany State Park.

There has been speculation that some of the Park founders intended it to be logged again. If that was the case, that intention did not find its way into law. Nowhere in the New York State laws governing Allegany State Park is there mention of timber management. The stated purpose of the Park in these laws is "for the recreation, instruction and health of the people."

In stark contrast, the laws that created the State Forests during the same period are very specific on the point of timber management. The Legislature used the language "forests which shall be forever devoted to the planting, growth and harvesting of trees."

Redhouse Saw Mill

Allegany's 67,000-acre forest is the only consolidated area of older growth forest in Western New York. There are 700,000 acres of forest in this area outside the Park which are being managed and harvested regularly. Another 500,000 acres to the south in Alleghany National Forest are being managed for timber. If Western New York is to have any older forest, Allegany cannot be cut down again.

The Adirondack Mountain Club believes that logging Allegany would be gravely detrimental to the regional diversity of our forests in Western New York. On the advice of our Legal Counsel, the Adirondack Mountain Club takes the stand that logging is clearly illegal in Allegany State Park.

Sincerely

Larry Beahan
Adirondack Mountain Club
Conservation Committee

52

Red House Lumber Yard

Adirondack Mountain Club, OPRHP
and
The Master Plan 1994

The meeting centered on the New York State Park System outside of the Adirondacks and particularly on Allegany State Park. This response on the part of the new York State Office of Parks and Historic Preservation and the ADK Headquarters staff to Niagara Frontier Chapter's request for help on Allegany was gratifying.

At the start Andy Beers, an Assistant Commissioner in Joan Davidson's OPRHP, spoke for half an hour and took questions for another half. He reviewed the massive New York State Park System for us (150 parks, 35 historical sites, 230,000 acres in all). He talked particularly about the 1993 Rockefeller report on the parks that found the infrastructure in sad disrepair, the budget, in real purchasing power, down 80% and staffing down 30% as compared to 1970. He told us of the considerable remedial efforts new Commissioner Davis has undertaken and left us feeling hopeful.

Beers was excellently informed about Allegany State Park and described it as a "hot bed of issues." Though he has responsibility for 130 parks, he knew the lumbering and gas and oil issues in Allegany almost as well as our own expert, Bruce Kershner.

He said that Commissioner Davis had promised to complete the Master Plan for Allegany "soon". At issue in the plan is whether the Park forests will be harvested for commercial use.

Beers and OPRHP seemed opposed to that idea but open to some "cutting for diversity." Neil Woodworth, counsel for ADK, stepped in and said that in his view there was a clear legal prohibition against commercial logging in the Park. I added that Western New York has all the cutover land and second growth in all stages that we can use. What we are lacking is the old growth that exists in only a few rare places like Allegany.

At this point Marilyn Gillespie, the current president of the Adirondack Mountain Club and active member of our own Niagara Frontier Chapter, made a moving speech about the importance of Allegany State Park to our Chapter and to herself personally. She talked of her family experiences there and made the statement, "I probably would not have had the interest in the outdoors that got me to be president of this club without Allegany."

I think we suitably impressed Beers with our interest. Beers went on to describe in detail the Oriskany Sandstone dome that National Fuel Gas has leased for gas storage. He talked about the sad fact that the Park's most valuable ecological asset, The BIG

TREE AREA, grows over the leased area. He said that OPRHP would like to have National Fuel out of Allegany State Park entirely and had taken them to court on their gas storage expansion proposal. OPRHP lost that decision and therefore is forced to cooperate with National Fuel.

In concluding, Beers urged ADK to pursue the protection of the Allegany's old growth forest. He said "National Fuel is vulnerable on the issue of its image as, `sensitive to nature'."

If environmental organizations like ADK can show the public that National Fuel is sacrificing an important ecological resource for profit, we might stop them yet.

After Commissioner Beers left, a motion was passed asking the Genesee and Niagara Frontier Chapters to get together and respond to this opening that Andy Beers offered. We are asked to prepare a resolution for the January meeting of the Conservation Committee stating the value of an intact climax forest in Allegany to the needed expansion of an outdoor recreation program for hiking and backpacking in the Park. This resolution, if passed by ADK's Board of Governors, would then tell National Fuel, OPRHP, the lumber industry and the public that 15,000 ADK outdoors-types heartily disapprove of anyone tampering with Allegany's woods.

Coyote Stuck in a Skull
Ogallala Lakota Trickster on the Allegany

Iktomi was a smallish male coyote, about three-and-a-half hands at the shoulder if you measured him generously with your fingers not tightly closed. Only a few patches of mange marked his rusty brown coat. A flash of white spread from his chest up both sides of his muzzle and leapt from there to his left forepaw. This white gave him a dashing air, of which he was justly proud. The pack alpha male took exception to that attitude and, when Iktomi showed a particular interest in a pure white female, he split Iktomi's right ear badly marring Iktomi's image.

So Iktomi had left with hurt feelings, a sore ear and unresolved pressure in his loins. He set off northward over prairie grasslands looking for a more receptive milieu for his appetites and his talents.

Iktomi traveled in hedgerows and mostly under cover of night. He had eaten a mouse two days before. All he had since then was a couple of grasshoppers and a taste of very poor raccoon scat. In the heat of the morning and until noon, he had slept in a culvert under the railroad. Two young boys in school uniforms discovered him there. They threw rocks at Iktomi and he had to run for his life.

Whenever Iktomi encountered other creatures he froze still until he understood whether he could eat them or they could eat him. He had seen a doe with two fawns and decided to give chase but he was all alone and so small that the doe turned and faced him down. He nearly got a nasty clip in the eye with one of her hooves.

One night on the banks of the Allegany far, far from his Black Hills home the moon rose full but clouds obscured the stars. The eerie shadows of the great forest made Iktomi nervous but still he could not restrain a lonesome howl. As the piteous cry reverberated in his upraised throat, he hoped and hoped that some poorly led pack would hear him and recognize him for the talented and randy top dog that he was. He was more afraid, though, that someone with a bow or an axe would hear. Still, after he gave in to his first long wailing cry, he could not resist an encore and then another.

Seneca Woman

Then he slunk off and broke into a rapid trot to fend off the chill of the night. As he moved with quick stealth through the shadows he thought, how pleasant it would be if I were back in the pack. If only I had had the sense not to let the boss sees me sniffing one of his bitches.

Today, how easy it would have been for the eleven of us to run down that doe and her fawns. What could I do alone? If the pack were here the Boss might have given me the nudge to lie in ambush while the rest of them drove the deer toward me. I would have leapt up out of the grass with such violence that she would have bolted in terror. I could have grabbed one of her delicious little beauties by the throat. My mouth is dripping saliva. Oh, I can taste the blood.

Then, he thought of what would have happened after, when they had eaten their fill. We would have gotten close together and howled at that lovely moon, what harmonies. Maybe I would have gotten to sleep next to Sheba, that sleek, all-white wonder. Oh, what torture. Sniff, sniff I think I can smell her.

Then, the next day if the doe hung around and we got her too, the Boss might call for a day of dancing and feasting. Like after the famous chicken house raid, when we were all prancing around and showing off. I did my forepaw dance and once I stayed up for a count of seven. No one in the pack had ever seen such a performance.

I was Chief!

Iktomi had learned that dance one night on a solo raid to an Ogallala encampment. His uncle had stolen an excellent pork chop from an old blind dog at that camp and bragged to Iktomi of the easy pickings.

Iktomi had circled the celebrating village, carefully avoiding the horses and the boy guarding them. His stiff walk and a very low growl had terrorized a scrawny pup that blundered into his stalking path. But Iktomi had become so entranced by the handstand dancing and the incessant drums that he neglected caution, and staring at the apparitions so precariously balanced, he stayed too long.

Iktomi recalled with a chill, those camp dogs must have picked up my scent or that pup, maybe he squealed. They were scouting me before first light. Didn't I have the dickens of a time getting away from that a big black sucker? He was two-thirds wolf and the rest, pissed-off bull buffalo.

With this turn of Iktomi's associations, they no longer comforted him. He realized again how homesick and lonely he was. He answered these feelings by moving faster. The exertion warmed him. He loved covering ground so quickly. Clouds came up and obscured the moon. The stars were even harder to see. Of course, with a nose and ears as excellent as Iktomi's, even with one ear split, he had no problem navigating

Then he heard it: a muffled drumming, a familiar beat, not unlike the one he had heard at the Ogallala camp. He had taken it home to the pack along with the trick of dancing on his forepaws. The pack had howled with delight and here it was again. But out here away from everything? He wondered. Am I losing it; could this be my imagination?

Hesitating, Iktomi lifted his white paw off the ground, pricked up his ears, sniffed, then locked on to the in-pouring sensory messages. He moved cautiously a step at a time away from the wagon ruts he had been following. He stopped by a large rock sniffed and lifted his leg. It was not so much that Iktomi had to relieve himself but that he felt he must assert to all passersby that someone was here with whom they would have to contend.

Then, feeling more confidence, Iktomi pursued the enticing sound. He leapt the muddy water in the ditch. He landed with unsteady footing in the midst of a heap of the ravaged bones of a long deceased buffalo; alongside the heap lay a mighty horned skull.

The skull was mostly bleached but had a greenish cast and quite a moldy odor. Shafts of scintillating light came from the eye sockets and nostril holes. This light illuminated the surrounding tall weeds creating flashes and shadows. The skull throbbed with beating drums. The rhythmic thumping of those drums and then that of hundreds of tiny feet of which he gradually became aware, were irresistible to the lonely traveler. The sights and sounds of such revelry filled Iktomi with a longing to join.

Looking closely at the skull, Iktomi found the outline of a tiny door on its forehead. With one claw of his dainty white forepaw, he tapped gently on the door. After several taps, he grew anxious and impatient, but mercifully a door mouse, tore himself away from the punch bowl and came to answer.

Iktomi's plea was so woeful that the tipsy door mouse took pity on him and checked with his supervisor. The supervisor, who was trying to pick up an attractive big-eared lady mouse in a minuscule skirt, did not bother to take a look for himself.

The door mouse came back saying, "It's okay. Come on in." He blinked and looked blearily at Iktomi and added, "But you are so big you gott'a use the back way."

Iktomi gratefully went to the hole at the back of the skull that had accommodated the buffalo's massive brain stem. There, with some effort, he was able to wriggle his head up inside.

Iktomi's head erupted through the base of the skull into the center of a dancing throng. Imagine how his canine teeth must have looked to the half-drunken mice dancing on the great floor of the buffalo's brainpan. As he became aware of these tasty morsels dancing all around his head, Iktomi's eyes rolled; he salivated; his jaws snapped reflexly.

The specter sent mice scurrying in panic. Their escape formed a sudden pity-patting wave as they frantically poured over one another, out the eye sockets, down the nostrils and from under the bony maxilla of the eternally patient buffalo.

Iktomi found himself not only alone and hungry but, now, crowned with a skull that was 12 sizes too large. He could barely lift his head from the ground for the weight of it. He went staggering back the way he had come. This time he splashed through the muddy water of the ditch instead of gliding lightly over it. As he reached the roadway, the great horned skull wagged and bumped until soon he was so tired that all he could do was to lie down and whimper.

A raccoon passed Iktomi and ignored his crying. A fox heard him and circled warily at a distance. A lioness sniffed him, but Iktomi smelled so bad of mouse piss that she decided not to eat him. Joe Whittaker came by and swore again to give up drinking his dinner in town. He muttered, "Imagine, a stupid dog with a Halloween mask."

Iktomi rolled to one side trying to relieve the cramp in his neck and glimpsed Old Grandfather Rock out of one corner of the buffalo's eye socket. He apologized to the ancient chunk of limestone, witness to the passing of ages. He said, "I'm sorry I didn't think to ask your permission before I left my mark on you but please could you help me? Get me out of this thing?"

Old Grandfather Rock chuckled, "Sure Iktomi, go ahead. Bang your skull against me all you want."

Iktomi swung his head hard against the gray rock with no result except for a resounding clang that echoed without mercy inside the buffalo skull and inside his own. He stood back, ran headfirst into the rock and got only more pain in his neck. Finally he combined these maneuvers and the skull fell away in shards. Iktomi staggered, his ears rang, his eyes swam, the night sky seemed to whirl about him but he was free.

The rock added a tale to his long repertoire.

And for several days Iktomi had the worst hangover of his life, they say.

Tunesassa
The Friends Indian School

To see Tunesassa go to the Friends Boat Launch on Route 280 along side Kinzua Reservoir just outside Allegany State Park. Walk into the stand of old evergreens near the water. You can still find a few massive blocks of masonry that are remnants of the Quaker School for Seneca Indians that operated there from 1798 to 1938. The school was, in a sense, a Marshall Plan to the Seneca Nation, more modest but similar to the assistance that the U.S. gave to Europe after WWII.

Towards the end of the Revolutionary War General George Washington dispatched General Sullivan and a contingent of the Continental Army on a punitive expedition against the Senecas. The Indians had sided in the war with their traditional allies, the British, and against the revolutionaries. To control the threat of their effective guerrilla warfare against his forces, Washington acted decisively and severely. Sullivan's men devastated the Seneca lands.

After the war Chief Cornplanter of the Senecas visited the capital, then at Philadelphia, and met several times with then President, Washington. There were proposals for the Senecas to move westward. Some of the Seneca's western allies continued to make war on the United States and tried to persuade Cornplanter and his people to join in that war.

Cornplanter refused. Instead, he agreed with Washington to keep the peace and in return his people received promises of certain benefits not all of which were honored. One landmark benefit that was delivered, however, was the interpretation of the American conquest of the British and their Seneca allies as a conquest of jurisdiction and not of ownership of Seneca lands.

As a result the Seneca are now among the few American Indians who live on land that they occupied when Columbus arrived.

The benefit that most concerns Tunesassa was the fulfillment of a joint request from Washington and Cornplanter that the Quakers of Philadelphia send technical assistance to the Senecas. The aid came in the form of the Friends Indian School at Tunesassa that, for 140 years, taught European ways of life and particularly European farming to generations of Senecas.

Religious educational missions to Indians have not fared well in the light of modern criticism. Such schools often uprooted their Indian students from traditional culture and their families. They left behind them trails of bitterness. This does not seem to be the case with Tunesassa. Perhaps that is because the school was physically near the heart of the Seneca Nation; perhaps because the Senecas invited help for a need in which at least some of them believed and perhaps it had to do with the character of Seneca and Quaker peoples.

To know what the school was really like, Judy Green, Director of the Seneca Museum in Salamanca, referred me to two former students of Tunesassa and to "Ne Ho Niyo De:No, That's what it was like" a collection of Seneca oral histories. Calvin John, who graduated in 1935, told me that his father sent him and later sent his two younger brothers there to learn dairy farming and that, "It was a good experience. We had to work hard. We lived on the basketball court. Our team was so good we could beat the men's team." Contrary to Quaker tradition and to the experience of some other alumnae, he said that the school used corporal punishment, "A hose, a club or a belt. They could dish it out." He also said that the school did not let them use the Seneca language there.

Dolores Jimerson, who graduated in 1918, told me, "I think it was great, but they didn't teach everything, no music. We had vacations summer and Christmas and our folks came to visit weekends. I could talk Seneca but not at school. They would never hit or whip you, just make you stand out in the hall."

Comments in the oral history were similar. Some students loved it, some were not so happy but the general tone of their responses was close to the way I felt about going to Parochial school in Buffalo. It was good for me, sometimes it was fun but it was a lot of work and the nuns were tough. But they only made us use Latin part of the time.

"A Quaker Promise Kept," written by Lois Barton who taught there one year, is the best overall description of Tunesassa that I found. It contains lists of students and faculty that go back to 1798 and many pictures. The Buffalo Historical Society has copies of brief histories of the school written in 1895 and 1914 by school administrators who provide a first-hand feeling about the place. Anthony Wallace's incomparable "Death and Rebirth of the Seneca," depicts the historical, political and sociological background for the story of the school.

I made an effort to discover the meaning of the word "Tunesassa." The librarian at Haverford College, which houses the Tunesassa School records, had no idea of its meaning. Hazel Dean-John, a Seneca linguist, could shed no light on it nor could the other Senecas whom I asked. Dwight "Deuce" Bowen gave the most authoritative interpretation I was able to find. He said, "Tunesassa just means the school. It don't mean nothing in Seneca. It's just a name. Some say it means 'dark waters' but if you say dark waters in Seneca it sounds nothing like that."

Since the name seems only to signify the school to the people who live near it and to those who went to school there, I am leaving it at that.

The historic marker, which the Allegany Historical Society has in mind, at this writing, has room for about fifty words. Our opinions have been shifting but I believe this is the current favorite formulation.

TUNESASSA
FRIENDS INDIAN SCHOOL

Quakers of Philadelphia, at the request of Seneca Chief Cornplanter and President Washington, operated a 692-acre model farm here with gristmill, sawmill, smithy, spinning and weaving shops and after 1852, a boarding school. Close to their homes, 40-50 young Senecas learned farming, homemaking and the three R's.

George Heron's
Tales of the Ga-hi-neh

Senecas, around Allegany, are often close mouthed about the ghostly lights, witches and unusual happenings reported in the Park just across the river from Cold Spring. So, when former Seneca Nation President, George Heron, started spinning yarns on the subject, we paid attention.

What follows is my recollection of George telling his Ga-hi-neh stories.

The occasion was an October 9th, 2000 hike to the Summit firetower organized by the Allegany State Park Firetower Restoration Committee. Tired and chilled from the hike in unexpected snow, our crowd of 20 children and adults were ready for stories. We settled back in the wood-paneled comfort of the Red House Administration Building and watched as our applause melted George's solemn face into a grin.

George is an older man, tall and dignified, with Indian looks. He came in wearing a tan fedora set squarely on his head, brim turned up all the way around, Indian style. He laid it and a camouflage jacket aside and stood before us dressed in green woolen shirt and khaki pants.

The Park that day was clothed in gold, red and orange, muted by an overcast sky. Patches of snow from an unseasonable storm highlighted the meadows and forest surrounding the lake. The storm had interrupted electric power for much of Salamanca and for Quaker Run. "I might be responsible for this bad weather," George said, hesitating. "Last night I burnt some tobacco. Indians always burn some tobacco before they start out to do anything. I let the smoke go up to the Creator to get his attention. I didn't think much of the summer we'd been having. So I guess he might of got sore and sent us some of this Indian summer." He paused, eyes twinkling, and we laughed.

"When they built the fire tower down here I was in the CCC, the Civilian Conservation Corps. I had all kinds of jobs around the Park but I never worked on the fire tower."

"The Government sent a man down here; we called him the `G-man.' He hired a guy in his sixties from over to the Nation to set up the I.D. That was the Indian Department. They went home every night. The rest had to stay in camp. I belonged to the regular CCC."

"That guy they put in charge, he appointed his son to run the I.D."

George confided, "Indians do like that, too, you know." The I.D. built the tower over on the reservation. Had to use a johnboat to haul the steel across the river. A johnboat is just a homemade boat with a blunt end on either end, just made up out of boards. Then they hauled the steel up the hill in a cart. The Government didn't just send down the G-man, you know. They sent down a horse, too. "George paused to let us know which was the higher regarded. Then he went on, "Anyone could use him to plow or haul lumber. His name was King. He pulled all that steel up the hill."

"The tower was a hundred feet tall. The one we looked at today was eighty-ninety foot. I never worked on them. I worked on a bigger one, the TV tower in Colden, 1250 foot tall. I worked on structural steel all my life. First day I looked down, I said, `What am I doing up here?' I got used to it. Got so I liked it."

George halted, kind of clearing his throat, "errgh," before starting in on his real subject; Ga-hi-neh. "There's a hill down here where you see Ga-hi-neh. They call it Bay State Hill. Coming west down the highway you can see it a long way coming. You don't know which way you'll get around it or if there's a tunnel through it. We live over in Cold Spring across the river. My Aunt Jenny could look out the window and tell the weather from the expression on its face. If it's scowling, `Look out, s'gonna' be bad weather.'"

"My uncle was born before the Civil War. He told me about them. About the Ga-hi-neh. It's like a light floating, too high to be a lantern. That would be down low, by your knee, if you were carrying it. Like a car headlight but with no explanation. And sometimes you might see a face in it, when it goes by."

"Three Indians were walking down that road. It was just a dirt road then, for a wagon or for horses. They met three Union soldiers. They were deserters trying to get away, up to Lake Erie. The soldiers asked the Indians to get them some food and some clothes. They said they would pay them. The Indians talked it over among themselves and agreed to do it, if they got paid. So the Indians brought back a bag of food and some overalls and things. Then the soldiers wanted directions to get up to the Lake. And the Indians told them how to get there."

"The soldiers had a bag full of gold coins, ten dollar gold pieces and whatever kind they had then. They said, 'Each of you can put a hand in and however many coins you can pull out you can keep them.'" George made a deep grasping movement with his big hand and grinned. Then his face fell as he said, "'But don't go spending the money right away. It's hot money.'"

"The soldiers went away and the Indians were left with their gold. The oldest one said, 'So, no one spends the money, give it all to me. I'll bury it back in by the Ga-hi-neh. I'll smoke my pipe and walk in there. When my tobacco is burned up and my pipe goes out, that's where I'll stop and bury the gold.' That's what they did and they all went home."

"That winter, the old one who buried the gold got sick. He died pretty quick, before he could tell them where it was. The other two tried to find the money. They smoked their pipes and walked till the pipes went out. They looked around for a big tree or something and they dug but they never could find it. One of them was Peter Jackson. His son was named Pete, too. Repeat." George halted here, smiling, and collected his laugh from the crowd.

"Young Peter Jackson used to go looking for it back there in Ga-hi-neh. I was a young kid then and I can remember going down to the store. Men would be hanging out there and when Pete went by they'd say, in Indian, (George gave us the Indian and then translated)'There's Peter Jackson gone looking for gold.'"

"Then the Pennsylvania Railroad built its river line down through there and that's where John Lanson had his cabin. He was a giant. I mean a real giant, not a tall skinny guy, a big man all the way round, seven feet tall. He used to travel round with the circus as the Wildman from Borneo. They'd throw a chicken in the cage with him and he'd eat the whole thing, alive. John died and they buried him back in there."

"That's not all that happened back there. Wait!"

"There was a railroad siding in there where you could fix a hot box or leave some loaded freight cars. A flagman was signaling the engineer. The engineer gave him four long toots, meaning he had one minute, and then two short ones, he'd better get on quick. The flagman shared the caboose with a conductor and a brakeman. When they got home they asked where the flagman was. He never got on. He disappeared."

"Well maybe he slid down the embankment," said George. But we all read his implication, something sinister happened.

"There was a guy over in Cold Spring. His aunt wanted some princess pine. He took a shovel and a bag and went over there to Ga-hi-neh where she said there was some and he was looking for ginseng too. It was getting dark and he saw something misty, and with a light, coming. When it hit him, he felt a warmth. It looked like a big man, a giant.

He ran. Lost his shovel and bag and everything. When he got to his aunt's house she looked at him and said in Indian (and he gave us the Indian,) 'You gone gray.'"

"They say there's a big snake in there. A man used to fish in the gravel pit left over from when they paired-up the Pennsy tracks. He liked to sit and smoke and rest. He always had a bobber. He'd just sit and watch. Once he was dozing. A rustling sound in the grass on the other side woke him up. It wasn't very wide there. He saw this snake 15-20 feet long. Nothing like that grows here. Maybe it escaped from a circus or maybe it ate something to make it grow like that. He ran home for his shotgun but, when he came back, he couldn't find it."

"Then one time there was a lot of sickness in Cold Spring. Someone had a dream about a fish. The fish said, 'Snakes are coming over from Ga-hi-neh and they are poisoning the water.'"

"They had good water there, that's why they called it Cold Spring. Everybody had their own well. Just dig down a little and there it was. Well, they got together and with their hoes and pitchforks they came over to Ga-hi-neh and they killed quite a few snakes. No really big ones. No 15-20 footers. The water got better. The sickness passed. Probably it was just a flood spoiled the water."

Oh, Yeah! we thought.

George went on, dead pan, "I saw a big snake once. I was in the Philippines on an L.S.T. We got a jeep to take a look around. Drove down this jungle road. Bump, bump we drove over a big Asian python. I told the driver, 'Quick back up, kill it.' Bump, bump again and then bump, bump. We looked back and there it was slithering off into the woods."

"I told the driver, 'Tell you what. You get out and tie a rope on his tail and we drag him back to the ship.' He looked at me and said, 'You all go to hell.'"

George got his best laugh out of that one.

"So now I'm hoping to catch the tail end of the Bills game. I think I talked enough. I'll quit now."

We all applauded. Our chairman thanked Mr. Heron and they shook hands.

My wife, Lyn, and I left the building with George. The sun had finally shone its face and when we three stepped into its warmth, George looked up smiling at the sky and said, "I guess, the Creator ain't mad at me anymore."

Wildcatting for Black Gold
Oil and Gas in Allegany

Webster's definitions:
Wildcat: verb, to search an area of unknown or doubtful productivity for oil.
Wildcat: noun, any of the North American felines of the genus Lynx.

Billions of square feet of natural gas and millions of barrels of oil have been brought up out of Allegany's deep underpinning rock. They have provided energy to run this country; they have given employment to many and wealth to a few. But there has been a cost to the Park. Its deep forest has been divided by a network of roads and in places is pocked with abandoned well.
Many would prefer deep intact forests. Many enjoy the trails.

History:
For starters, here are some clips from the SALAMANCA PRESS:

October 27, 1922: "WELL MAY BE BEST IN RED HOUSE OIL REGION Following the shooting of the well, three spurts of apparently nearly pure oil rose to a height of 15 to 25 feet above the top of the derrick. The well is located on a lease on the former McCapes farm. The oil-bearing sand lies a little more than 1,300 feet below surface level."
July 15, 1939: "75 SEE OIL WELL SHOT ON LEASE IN STATE PARK Visitors to Allegany State Park this morning had a chance to see one of the most spectacular phases of the oil industry... 120 quarts of nitroglycerine were set off in the 1,200 foot deep well on the Bates property." Neville France was reported as "the operator of the lease."
December 9, 1955: "FLOW OF WILDCAT GAS WELL IN PARK ESTIMATED AT 8 MILLION CUBIC FEET The well is located between camps 10 and 12- Carleton and Arrowhead – on

the west side of Red House Valley. It is on a tract of approximately 1,000 acres purchased by the Park from the Lockwood estate of Randolph, which retained mineral rights...Known as the Lena Lockwood No. 1, the wildcatter was drilled by the Felmont Oil Corp."

Hook France, a retired Park ranger, long-time Park resident and undoubtedly a relative of Neville France mentioned in the 1939 item above, recalls an old time Red House farmer who got sick on the day that a big well finally blew in on his property. In the excitement someone got him horse liniment, for medicine, by mistake. The farmer swallowed a dose, then stared at the label and exclaimed, "Oh my God, it's the day I got rich and the same day I'm gonna die."

We campers had no idea of the churnings of the oil industry that were going on around us or that had gone on in the Park before.

I was a camper at Camp 12 in 1939 when it was called Camp Bee Tee Vee. Park roads were mostly gravel in those days and the trees were sixty years shorter. We had no idea they were shooting off nitroglycerine next door or we would have snuck over to watch. I came back as a counselor in 1953 when Camp 12 had changed its name to Arrowhead. That was just, two years before the Lena Lockwood blew in. Today on Allegany State Park Highway One in Red House, between camps 10 and 12 you can see green sheds that house gas-pumping equipment for National Fuel.

Four hundred million years ago, in the time geologists call the Devonian period, Allegany began its petroleum story. The Park was under a sea. The tectonic plate of earth crust on which it stands was then in the Southern Hemisphere drifting north. Mud and sand sea-bottoms layered down on one another, through the ages. Their weight compressed them into rock. Embedded in those rock layers were the organic remains of sea life: fish, plants and masses of microscopic organisms. Eons of pressure and heat processed them into hydrocarbons, Allegany's black gold, petroleum.

The ancient sea bottom is evident on the Park road down from the Summit Ski Area on toward Salamanca. Layers of gently wave-marked sandstone and others filled with brachiopods, trilobites and other fossils are exposed at cuts like at Sweet Water Spring along the way. The great boulders of Thunder Rock were once sea-bottom.

In 1627, the French missionary, D'Allion, visited Indians of the tribe called Neutrals, at Oil Spring near present day Cuba, New York. D'Allion's observation of Indian use of the oil as a medicine is the first indication of European awareness of American petroleum. The Seneca Nation still owns a mile-square reservation at Oil Spring and for many years petroleum was know as "Seneca oil." Visitors there can see the spring encased in an ancient wooden wall preserved by impregnation with oil.

In 1859 Colonel Edwin Drake drilled the first commercially successful oil well in the world at Titusville, Pennsylvania 30 miles southwest of Allegany State Park. Soon John D. Rockefeller moved in and began his fortune by converting petroleum to kerosene, which replaced whale oil and candles for the illumination of the world. There is a replica of Drake's engine house and oil derrick in the oil museum at Titusville now.

In 1864, within the present boundaries of Allegany State Park, Job Moses drilled New York State's first commercial oil well. A granite monument near its site commemorates Moses and this event. To find it, take the Park Limestone Road toward Limestone three-and-four-tenths miles past its intersection with the Thunder Rock-Ridge Road. The monument is there on the right. If you don't see it, ask at one of the homes along the road. Yes, it is not well known but many lucky people live on private land in the Park.

Limestone became a boomtown with the discovery of oil. Little Ireland, its farming-village neighbor, whose remnants are still on the eastern slope of Allegany State Park, did not fare so well. Waldo Peternatti wrote in the Bradford newspaper, Era, "John Carmody (of Little Ireland) was one of the most prosperous oilmen, boasting six oil wells for which he was paid a royalty of 1/8-percent net of the oil produced. The foundation of his home is still intact today and in good condition considering it was laid 130 years ago." Peternatti tells us that Little Ireland, a colony of transplanted Irish canal-diggers-turned-farmers, had its fields explored for oil and its people dispersed to work in near and distant oilfields.

I tracked down the foundations of four houses on my hike to Little Ireland. They are to the right and left of Irish Brook Road, which is now a horse trail that leads north from the Limestone Road tollbooth. The remains of the village are a half-hour or so's walk down this trail. If you come to the three-tiered beaver pond, you have just passed it.

Job Moses Monument

By 1878, two-hundred-and-fifty New York State oil wells were producing, mostly in Cattaraugus and Allegany Counties.
In the 1890's, gas and oil pools of English Brook, Rice Brook and Red House were developed inside what is now the Park. Eventually there were over 200 wells drilled in the Park. Depleted wells got new leases on life with modern techniques of extraction

like flooding old wells. The addition of water allowed residual oil to float higher and be extracted.

In the 1920's, during the time that the Park was being created many landowners that sold property to the Park held on to mineral rights. Park administrators have had to keep that in mind as they planned the future of the Park.

In 1931, there were only 5 producing oil wells in Allegany State Park. But Robert Moses, then, Chairman of the NYS Council of Parks and architect of much of the park and highway system of New York State, was concerned about Park mineral rights. He ordered an investigation, raising the question whether Allegany, so encumbered by gas leases and privately owned mineral rights, was a suitable place for the State to invest Park funds. George Ansley, Salamanca member of the Allegany State Park Commission, roundly condemned him and the Park went on.

Gas installation on ASP 2

In the 1950's, Felmont Oil Company found gas at 6,000 feet in Red House's Oriskany sandstone. A few years later when the gas was exhausted, they converted those wells to storage of natural gas. This storage system provided an uninterrupted supply of gas required for their operation of a chemical plant in Olean.

In 1981, during the world wide energy crunch, Allegany and virtually all State forests and parks were opened up for gas and oil exploration. By 1984, Allegany State Park Director Hugh Dunn reported ten miles of new road and 30 new wells in operation in the southeastern corner of the Park. Felmont took a State lease on 9000 acres in the center of the Park and was driving more deep wells for gas. Despite the urgent need for energy sources, Park officials held drilling operators to high standards of environmental care and the new roads were slated eventually to become trails.

In 1990, Felmont sold National Fuel Gas, its system of storage wells, which were tapped into the gas pipeline that crossed the eastern part of the Park carrying gas from Pennsylvania northward.

The situation today is:

1. National Fuel operates its cross-park pipelines and 14 storage wells to collect stores of gas in summer and dispense them in colder months. As part of the rent for their 9,000-acre lease off France Brook Road, they supply the Park with gas to heat the Red House Administration Building. They have publicized an intention to expand gas storage in the Park.

2. Another company has six oil wells in operation in the southeastern corner of the Park.

3. There remain unknown resources in both the explored and unexplored areas of the Park. Mineral rights to about a third of those are in private hands.

During the big boom, in the 1890's there was a circuit-riding preacher who horse-backed on his rounds in the oil fields to exhort against the oil boom. "The Lord stored oil in the earth to fuel the fires of hell," he warned. "To remove it is sinful and the world will feel His wrath."

Opinion remains divided on the blessings of petroleum. In Allegany State Park the bulk of oil and gas exploration appears to be over. Perhaps the deep-forest-loving, real wildcats will now be willing to take a chance on the Park again.

Friends of Allegany Meets National Fuel Gas Dec. 29, 1994

National Fuel Gas invited fifteen members of a coalition of environmental groups called Friends of Allegany to meet with three of their staff in that Gas Company's headquarters in downtown Buffalo. The idea was to give a "reassuring update" on their proposal to expand natural gas storage in Allegany State Park. On the Gas Company side of the table sat Art Coon, Public Relations, Ron Kramer, their Engineer for Allegany, and Dave Bimber, Supervisor of Construction. Bruce Kershner led the Friends contingent.

The Gas Company calls its Allegany gas storage field, Limestone. It, together with Callen Run in Pennsylvania, comprises this gas storage capacity expansion effort which they call the Laurel Fields Project. Allegany's present capacity is 2.9 billion cubic feet top gas (gas storage volume above that necessary to create pressure to operate the wells). They wish to expand it to 7. Last year the target was 6. The pressure would be at 2100 pounds per square inch which is the original pressure of gas in the Oriskany sandstone formation there. Callen Run has a capacity of 12 billion cubic feet. A 60-mile pipeline would be needed to connect the two.

The Gas Company began physical preparation for the expansion of gas storage in Allegany State Park in September 1993. They deepened 5 wells in the Park and charted the geological structures of 3. These studies led to abandoning 2 wells in the Park to the east of Allegany State Park Highway 2. They moved the area of proposed development south and west in the Park so that at least two wells would be located across or south of France Brook and France Brook Road. A connecting pipeline would have to cross France Brook.

Gas Company has assured the Park that they will not find it necessary to drill in the drainage of Stoddard Creek. Stoddard

Creek is in the heart of the Big Tree Area and drains into Red House Lake.

They had planned 14 new wells. They are now planning 16 wells. They plan 7 new well-head sites. These will be largely in the area now designated as the Big Tree area. If they are not in it they are quite close to it.

At this point the Gas Company presented the centerpiece of their offer to have concern for the environment in these "Laurel Fields." To address the complaints the Park, Friends of Allegany and others had presented, they offered us assurance that they would plan to use angle drilling and run two wells from each well-head.

Still, a main stem collector pipeline would be cut through the Big Tree area with collectors from each of the well-head sites. They want to place a mile of this pipeline on the North Country Trail, itself.

In the course of construction, 116 acres of forest would be cleared. 41 of those acres would be new permanent clearings. They gave us a mileage figure for new pipelines and roadways in the Big Tree area but I missed it.

Pipeline K runs 11 miles north and south through the Park parallel to Allegany State Park Highway 2. Its southern half would be widened for the installation of a new line. A new 5-acre compressor station would be installed in the Park near Limestone. A new 12-inch line would be run alongside the existing one to that station.

That pipeline would pass directly through Thunder Rock.

NFG has completed their Federal Energy Regulatory Commission application but the Feds have not responded. The Gas Company will make copies of the application available to Friends.

They own 32 gas storage fields in Western New York and Pennsylvania for a total capacity of 125 billion cubic feet. If the project goes through, the Gas Company would set up a new corporation to own the "Laurel Fields" (Laurel Fields, doesn't that make a bunch of oily pipes in clear-cut patches of woods sound wonderful?) and related pipelines. They are looking for a partner corporation to bring capital and new customers into the deal. At present they do not have enough customers signed to justify the

Allegany portion of the project to the Feds, let alone the Callen Run portion. They do expect enough customers for Allegany soon. They will be primarily in New England and New Jersey and the Midwest.

From a practical physical point of view the full capacity of a field must be developed for it to work at all as a storage field. One of the biggest expenses is pumping in gas to create pressure that will expel the storable or "top gas." The Feds at FERC will not allow anyone a profitable rate based on the partial use of a gas storage field's capacity. Since sufficient customers aren't as yet available to make it pay and the Gas Company prefers not to wait, it has withdrawn Callen Run and plans to go ahead only with the field in Allegany State Park.

The total cost of the combined Laurel Fields project would come to about $125 million. $5 million has already been spent on development and $9 million on acquiring the lease in Allegany. A total of $49 million would be spent on the Allegany portion of the project.

The State of Pennsylvania is eager to have Callen Run developed in its state forest because of the revenue. The Gas Company would have had to pay them $180,000 per year for the 12 billion cubic feet of storage there. They would pay New York State only $36,000 per year for the 7 billion cubic feet they plan in Allegany. That is $ 5142 per BCF in Allegany and $15,000 per BCF at Callen Run.

Another $24,000 rental is scheduled for pipelines. This makes a total of $235,000 in proposed rentals.

There are other potential gas storage fields nearby such as State Line in Allegany County which has a capacity of 50 million BCF. Its chief drawback is, as pointed out above, the whole 50 million BCF would have to be used all at once. The field has not been studied in detail to be certain that it would work well for storage but it is promising.

The Gas Company does not expect the Park draft Environmental Impact Statement to be released quite as imminently as was recently indicated to Friends of Allegany. It will probably be this spring.

Ordinarily federally approved plans like this are exempt from the New York State Environmental Quality Review act

(SEQR). However the Gas Company's lease required that if it went beyond 4 BCF of storage they would have to meet or better SEQR standards.

The Gas Company has hired Ecology and Environment to study the impact of their proposal on flora and fauna. Dr. Chris Nowak, formerly of the US Forest Service, is studying the Old Growth forest. Robert Zirimba is doing the botany.

The Gas Company lease was recently renewed but is not automatically renewable at the end of the next twenty years. The Park and the New York State Department of Environmental Conservation (DEC) have expressed grave concerns about its exercise of this lease and have given no apparent assurance that it would be again renewed. Still the Gas Company seems intent on investing $49 million In Allegany State Park.

They interpret the recently renewed lease to allow them not only to continue their current storage operation but to expand it. Their conclusion does not necessarily follow according to the reading of lawyer members of Friends of Allegany who were present. This question has not been tested in court.

A court action brought by the New York State Office of Parks and Historic Preservation (OPRHP) against them as lease holders did give them access to an 880-acre buffer zone around the lease area bringing the total lease area to 9140 acres. This was upheld on appeal.

The Gas Company complained of OPRHP's unwillingness to discuss what might be done in mitigation for their proposed disturbance of the forest. Friends of Allegany also declined to discuss mitigation.

CONCLUSIONS:

1. There are gas storage fields that are alternatives to Allegany.

2. The proposed expansion in Allegany State Park from 2.9 to 7 BCF is only 3% of the present gas storage capacity the gas Company has in this region.

3. The Gas Company proposes to deface Allegany State Park to take advantage of an archaic lease. That lease of gas storage space would pay NY State at 1/3 the going market rate.

4. Even with the modification of angled drilling, the proposal disrupts a third of the Big Tree area with roads, new well heads and pipelines.

5. The pipeline changes in the proposal tear up Thunder Rock, the North Country Trail and the meadows along Allegany State Park Highway 2.

6. The Gas Company almost completed its Federal Energy Regulatory Commission application without any opportunity for comment from NY State or any environmental group.

7. This National Fuel Gas Company is vulnerable on their slogan, "Working to protect the Environment for 100 years."

8. Very little of the proposed gas storage would benefit Western New York.

9. There must be a way for rate structures or federal regulations to be modified or a consortium to be formed to make legal the use of the larger gas fields that exist outside of Allegany.

I told the National Fuel Gas guys that their suggestion of slant drilling was like offering us a really nice funeral, if we let them cut out our heart.

National Fuel Gas
"Go Take a Hike"

Representative Jack Quinn
331 Cannon House Office Building
Washington DC 20515

Jan. 1, 1995

Dear Jack,

Please take a look at this article. It outlines a threat to the forests of Allegany State Park. National Fuel Gas's application is now before the Federal Energy Regulatory Commission.

Please consider voicing your opposition to this destruction of "the Crown Jewel of the New York State Park system" by contacting Laura Turner at FERC (202) 208 0916.

Sincerely
Larry Beahan

National Fuel Gas has asked New York State permission to triple its underground natural gas storage in Allegany State Park. That operation already disrupts part of the old-growth forest in the center of the Park.

The heart of the Park is a triangle bounded by Allegany State Park Highway 1, Allegany State Park Highway 2 and France Brook Road. That heart is the Big Basin and its Big Tree area. They are a maturing mixed hardwood forest of 90-year-old trees and a glorious 900-acre stand of old-growth. The 350-year-old hemlocks in the Big Tree Area are still mostly intact. They had never seen an axe, till the gas and oil people came along.

Now, National Fuel Gas wants to cut down 12 more acres of this old-growth, to double its number of storage wells from 14 to 29. The road cutting, pipeline laying and well-drilling would drastically change the character of 220 more acres of this irreplaceable forest.

Big Basin has the largest old-growth forest in Western New York. Its isolation and maturity provides a needed refuge for black bear, Pileated woodpeckers, hawks and song birds. Even deep-forest dwellers like lynx and fishers could live there.

The industrial expansion which National Fuel Gas proposes would affect more than the Park's heart. To rebuild one pipeline, they would cut an 11-mile-long, 45-foot-wide swath parallel to ASP 2 and another, east, toward Limestone, to a compressor station. They would expand the compressor station to occupy five acres of Park.

National Fuel Gas is a big, profitable, nationwide company. In six years their stock has risen from 20 to 35 dollars. In each of those years their dividend rate has gone up. Still, they advertise themselves as an "environmentally friendly" company.

Indeed, their corporate policy says, "National Fuel Gas will conduct its operations in a manner consistent with: respect for, protection of, and improvement of our environment."

Why then, does National Fuel Gas select the pristine forests of Allegany State Park for the expansion of their commercial interests? They own 30 other underground gas storage fields. Why expand one in an old-growth forest?

Maybe it's the cheap rent. They bought their Allegany lease from Felmont Oil in 1990 for $9 million. They pay New York only one third of one percent of that for rent, $30,000.

In October 1993 the New York State Office of Parks, Recreation and Historic Preservation, (OPRHP) and National Fuel Gas complied with the law that requires public consultation before beginning such a project. They held two scoping sessions which were the only widely-publicized announcements of their intentions.

Sometime last fall, before the public could speak out at these sessions, OPRHP allowed National Fuel Gas to send their crews to work in Big Basin. National Fuel Gas graded the roads, reopened grown-over clearings, deepened five wells and tested three more. They tore up the woods. This jumping-the-gun they called, "a project to further evaluate...gas storage...in the Park."

I took a walk through the gas storage fields to get a first-hand look. I hope readers will invite decision-makers from the NYS Legislature and OPRHP to take this walk with them.

Gas storage well, off France Brook Road

On the way to France Brook Road, I drove south on ASP 2 from Red House toward Thunder Rock. I stopped halfway between Camp Carleton and Camp Arrowhead. There the lease reaches down from the hills in the center of the Park, into the valley and spills across the highway.

Two of National Fuel's gas wells are there, by the side of the road. They are covered by peculiar, little, green-painted sheds and surrounded by large gravel pads. In the meadow opposite them, there is a complex of pipes, which National Fuel Gas has not bothered to conceal, in any way. The gas storage lease allows Park authorities to require National Fuel Gas to bury equipment that can be seen from a road or a trail. Why not these?

To get to the main gas field, park at the barrier on France Brook Road and walk west. The road to the wells comes in from the north, three-quarters of a mile from ASP 2. It climbs steeply through dense stands of large maple, hemlock, beech and white pine. There are prime black cherry trees two feet in diameter. Along that road, one old beech has bear claw scars, little ones, the size a cub would make. The grand daddy of all

Pileated Woodpecker's work on a dead tree

woodpeckers, the seventeen-inch, isolation-loving Pileated woodpecker, has left his telltale mark in a dead tree, a gaping quadrangular hole three by twenty-four inches. With all the traffic, that wary bird won't be back here to search for grubs.

Many times that afternoon I saw the forest maimed by branching and re-branching roads, vacant space and metal fixtures. At the well farthest north, a circling Goshawk warned me away from her nest with an angry, "kak-kak-kak-kak-kak."

That Goshawk's message must get to the New York State Office of Parks and Historic Preservation, National Fuel Gas, and the NYS Legislature.

Park for Sale, Cheap

Want to buy Allegany State Park? National Fuel Gas (NFG) seems to. A friend of mine who happens to be a friend of the Town of Red House assessor tipped me off. In February of 1997, NFG quietly purchased the mineral rights to 344 acres of Allegany State Park just off ASP 2 over near Camp Arrowhead and Camp Carrolton. NFG tracked down the owner somewhere in Texas. They paid him just under $5 an acre for it, $1645.

NFG now owns the right to do whatever they have to do, on that one-half-square-mile of Park, to make use of their new mineral rights. They can cut roads, bar the roads with iron gates, drill wells and put in pumps and pipelines. They may leave wells there forever, if they decide to use it for storage. They have done that with 9000+ acres up France Brook Road.

I called NFG's public relations office to see if they would share their intentions. They would not. Their spokesperson said only that NFG has an ongoing interest in Allegany State Park.

Well, so do I, and so do the half million annual visitors to the Park from Erie and Niagara Counties. We helped pass the 1.75 billion dollar Clean Water/ Clean Air Bond Act. One hundred and fifty million dollars of that was set aside to buy "Open Space."

In February of 1997, just as NFG was buying that piece of Allegany State Park, Western New York's Region 9 of the Department of Environmental Conservation (DEC) convened a committee to advise on open space to be purchased. Mineral rights in Allegany State Park placed among their 12 top recommendations along with Motor Island, the Ellicott Creek Water Way, DeVeaux Woods and others.

I went back to the next meeting of that committee a year later on February 19 of this year. DEC representatives greeted the committee with Bluebird Posters and the great news that the State had purchased one of the committee's top-priority pieces, Motor Island in the Niagara River. Motor Island, with its wild heron rookeries, is an excellent addition to our parks, though at $250,000 for 31 acres, its $8000 per acre is mighty pricey in comparison to NFG's deal down in the Park.

Most of the committee members were not aware of NFG's purchase in the Park. When they found out about it several of them demanded to know how this could happen and urged action on the part of the DEC and of Allegany State Park.

A DEC representative responded, "Buying these rights is a very complex business." He admitted that the DEC had no program for it. He tossed a lateral to ex-Buffalo Bill, Ed Rutkowski, and now Director of the State's Niagara Region Parks. Rutkowski had nothing in his playbook to handle this NFG offense but he caught the ball. He asked for my copy of NFG's Quit-Claim-Deed to their new holdings, which I gladly provided him. He promised to respond.

Now, it would help if about a thousand people would telephone and write Mr. Rutkowski urging him to take action. We need a full-time real estate office in the Niagara District Parks directed to buy up the mineral rights to the half of Allegany State Park that are still in private hands. "Eminent Domain" might be a reasonable thing to consider as well.

On December 12 of 1955 a newspaper headline blared, "Big Gas Well In State Park Muzzled".

The article went on: "The wildcat well that blew in Thursday in Allegany State Park with an estimated daily flow of more than eight million cubic feet of gas was muzzled yesterday about noon. About a thousand sacks of sticky barium sulphate were used along with a lot of drilling mud to stop the flow after three days of virtual round-the-clock work..."

1955 does not seem very long ago to me. It was just two years after my wife and I spent the summer counseling at Camp Arrowhead. They were talking about a gas well right next door to our camp and very close to the piece to which NFG has just purchased rights.

Allegany State Park itself has a policy against exploiting any remaining gas or oil reserves that it owns within its boundaries. NFG is bound by no such policy. Our main chance here is if Ed Rutkowski scores with this one.

Halloween
at
Valentine's

This is a story about a place in Allegany State Park I have never heard mentioned by any official nor have I seen any actual sign of this "Valentine Retreat." As to whether or not there is any truth to the alleged occurrences there, I can make no statement except that the December issue of the Salamanca Republican that supposedly made reference to them could not be found. Here is the way the story was told to me by a person who wishes to remain unnamed.

Always edgy, Peter Hare (Hare was not Peter's actual last name) listened skeptically as Pastor Bill, the sinewy minister with the whaler's beard and the nonchalant laugh, finished his welcoming speech. "You are all going to have a swell time here at the Valentine Retreat and Nature Center. Our food is terrific, all God's Allegany State Park nature is here for you and one special couple among you will have the wonderful opportunity of renewing their marital vows to climax this special Halloween Elderhostel at Saint Valentine's own special spot here in just about the nicest park in the world, our own Allegany." He ended in a crescendo and the guests responded with vigorous applause and a few whistles. Peter didn't stir.

"Oops," Pastor Bill exclaimed, "almost forgot to do it. I have to formally turn you over to your caretaker for this week. Here is the inimitable, the only, the wonderful David "Big Bird" Raptor, your naturalist, guide and keeper." David, a tall gangly man with a great nose and very little chin, stood up grinning. He raised both arms and waved them like a giant pair of wings and let out a cry halfway between that of a chicken and a peacock, "cock-a-doodle-squawk," and everybody laughed with him, as he waved them toward the bus. "Come on, no time to talk, we got a boat trip on Kinzua Reservoir and we're late."

Peter was alarmed and almost opted out of the trip when, during boarding the boat, a passenger, a chubby, former school teacher, jibed at the Captain, "Careful of the crocodiles now."

"Don't you worry," he replied with a wink. "I've done this trip once or twice, you know."

David hauled in the gangplank, then turned to the group and said, "We may not have crocodiles but it is possible that you may see an Allegany Hellbender. More of a large salamander than an alligator but some of them run up to three feet long. Keep your eyes pealed and your fingers inside the boat."

"Oh my God, what have I got myself into?" thought Peter as the Captain at the wheel in the stern gently edged the throttle of the twin 200-horsepower Johnson motors forward. The canopied, twin-hulled raft, with its load of white plastic tables and chairs filled with Elderhostel guests, edged away from Friends Boat-launching Ramp and out into the center of Kinzua Reservoir.

Peter Hare was not comfortable in boats. He glanced around, looking for the life jackets and wishing that he could put one on, though he wondered what good they would do in Hellbender-infested waters.

Peter shivered as he sat on the open deck of the Kinzua Tour raft. The sun shone coldly on the blue waters and the reds and yellows of its forest shore. October was cold in Allegany country. "Why didn't I go to Florida he grumbled to himself," as he pulled a thin cotton sun hat down over his balding head and wished he had brought his Norwegian ski cap with the ear-lappers.

David smiled benignly at Peter from behind his great, long beak of a nose. Peter, wanting to get his money's worth, had been careful to sit near this tall, awkward nature expert who was teaching the environmental courses at the Valentine Retreat Center Elderhostel. But David was letting the Captain guide do most of the talking.

"No, we have no crocodiles here, only very rarely. What we do have is Hellbenders. There is one right over there," he said, coasting the raft silently against the shore. Peter was startled to see a brown object that he had taken for a small log, paddling smoothly, almost at his elbow.

Peter shrunk away. David whispered to him, "Not to worry. He's too cold to eat you."

Arnold, the Renaissance Art teacher, who had brought along his slender, vacuous wife, alternated with the chubby school teacher in bombarding David with questions. "What do Hellbenders eat? What is that bird? What are those trees?" David smiled equally benignly on each of them and motioned to the Captain for the answers who, having the mike in hand, took over.

"Look at that Great Blue Heron off the bow. "

Peter now wished he had sat up forward, as the collection of skinny and fat, gray and dyed-headed Elderhostelers wrapped in assortments of improvised clothes against the weather, rose for the view and obstructed his. Arnold helped his wife, Kitty, up, pointing in the direction the guide indicated. "See, there he is, Honey." Peter remained in his seat and stared at both of their backs.

"Where, Arnold? I don't see anything" Kitty replied in her patient, uncaring voice. But the heron, the gawky, lean bird, in whom Peter saw some resemblance to David, took a few wading steps and launched himself gracefully into the air. The large, blue-gray bird, long neck folded and legs extended straight back, soared alongside the boat, right past and a little too close to where Peter sat in his chair. The bird landed in the swampy waters and eyed Peter with what seemed to Peter, menace.

Peter shrank back again and cast a glance at David. The tall, quiet man shook his head and smiled as he winked at the chubby teacher who then smiled. Arnold, seeing those smiles, smiled at Kitty who always smiled. Peter felt there was some kind of smiling and winking conspiracy, though he knew, at least, that Kitty wasn't in on it.

The Captain guide drove the boat out into mid-stream. "Whoops, did you see him? That beaver dove right under us and headed for his lodge over by the shore. There's a Bald Eagle in that dead tree. The Great Blue Heron you just saw is one of our biggest birds."

Someone asked, "What do heron's eat?"

"Well, a great Blue's favorite food is a snake. They get them out here and they swallow them whole. They like to swallow them headfirst. Of course, they like them dead when they swallow them so they hold them in their beak just behind the head so the snake can't reach around and bite them. They strangle them and then swallow them. You can see that big, long snake travel like a string of spaghetti down his long, skinny neck"

Peter gulped. The guide's image was too explicit. He could see the struggling snake gradually succumbing and the great bird flipping it into its gullet and swallowing, the snake's head making a bulge in the bird's throat as the body followed down. The tail hung out of the beak 'til the bird jerked his head and inhaled the last of it. Nature is vicious, Peter thought, and his mind turned to the wife who had left him for a richer, younger, less anxious man 20 years before. He imagined her being swallowed by a Hellbender and he didn't feel so bad.

"They like rats about second only to snakes. They pick them up by the tail and with that long, powerful neck of theirs they'll snap them around into a rock or a stump and kill them before they swallow them. If they are out here away from a rock or anything, they wade out a little, holding the rat by the tail, and dangle him with his head under water 'til he's drowned."

Peter frowned at Arnold, looking for support for his disapproval, his horror at what was being described. Arnold returned only a blank look as he wiped Kitty's nose and said to her, "That's how they feed the herons, Honey."

"Thank you, Arnold," she replied sniffling. Mercifully for Peter the cruise ended shortly.

Part of the deal was lunch at a tiny restaurant over near Limestone to which they were taken in a slick, new bus with its own toilet. The bus just barely negotiated the bumpy Limestone road causing Peter many palpitations.

Once there, Peter sat at the table that was served last. He accepted that injustice as his typical lot. He declined the Hellbender sandwich even though David had explained that it was only deep-fried catfish. He settled for a green salad, a roll and apple juice. You'd think that in cider country you could get cider, he griped to himself.

He retired to one corner of the table as best he could. There he absorbed himself in the copy of Thoreau's "Walden" which he had sworn he would finish on this trip though he had had this book and this intention ever since his wife's departure. The chubby school teacher sat uncomfortably close to him but finally gave up trying to draw him into conversation.

David entertained the crowded restaurant by swallowing whole an eleven-inch pickled eel and then stood at the counter swallowing a huge mock Hellbender sandwich in great chunks as Arnold and Kitty sat on tall stools and nibbled alongside him. Arnold kept on with running observations of his on the trip and the world. He topped it off by doing, for the whole restaurant, a mildly bawdy vaudeville-comedy routine that wound up in a song called "Tapioca."

Finally, the magnificent bus returned them by superhighway to the Valentine Retreat Center grounds. The bus's back-up beeper continued to pierce the air of the conference grounds as Peter escaped the elder mob. This was his first Elderhostel. He had dreaded the idea of declaring himself that old, but the price was so economical he could finally not resist.

The sun was setting in a marvelous golden hue behind the autumn-hued mountain, into which the Valentine Retreat Center's main meeting and dining building nestled. Peter climbed into the two-person swing suspended from a giant maple on the lawn. He gazed languidly at the bigger-than-life concrete cross, with its great Saint Valentine's heart at the intersect now scintillating in the rays of the sun. The vivid cross was reflected in the waters of a reed-outlined pond. Peter found the cross depressing. The sun seemed to warm the chilling air and it provided this golden light. He opened Thoreau once more and began to read.

Arnold and Kitty walked by waving and murmuring. They joined another couple on the lawn chatting gaily, pointlessly. Peter buried his head in the book as the school teacher brushed close by on her way to join the group, which was so dramatically back-lit against the sun. David arrived and the throng gathered around his tall, silhouetted figure.

The gathering distracted Peter. What is going on, he wondered? There wasn't any announcement. The gathering felt ominous to him. All that yellow light, the cross, the unreal shapes against the sun and a rustle of speech just outside his range of hearing. He wanted to shout a warning.

David, who stood out head and shoulders above the others, looked almost surrounded in halo. He led them away, teaching as they walked. He stopped now and again pulling down a branch, picking up a seed or a stone, showing it in his outstretched hand and expounding.

Peter could contain himself no more. Should I call 911? he thought. Something is not right. I should jump in my rental car and get away from here. That's what I should do. But he did not.

He slammed his book closed and tiptoed off to one side of the path concealing himself in the brush as, in his younger days, he had read of Indians doing. He kept his distance as he shadowed the elder cluster. Once David stopped and looked right through Peter. Peter froze, until David turned and led the group out of sight. When it felt safe, Peter took up this stalking again.

They were gathered in the reeds, by the cross when, through orange and yellow foliage, Peter could see them once more. The dozen or fifteen elderly people in their tennis shoes and plaid trousers, their baseball caps and crimson cloaks stood awed in silence. The only sound to be heard was that of Kitty squealing in confused disbelief. Towering, David had picked her up by the left foot and waded knee deep into the lake. He held his right hand high in the air and from it, dangling upside down by one foot, her gray head bobbing in and out of the water, flapped poor Kitty.

She gave a final twist and hung still. To Peter's horror David flipped Kitty into the air and swallowed her headfirst. He swallowed several times, choked a little and pushed but she finally slipped down inside his gullet. At the last second her left sneaker, a little white one popped off. David caught it adroitly and flipped it down after her.

Trembling, Peter slipped quietly into the forest, got in his rented Honda and sped away. After returning home he immediately called the Salamanca Republican and asked, "Have you had any extraordinary news from Allegany State Park in the last few days?"

The operator said, "No, nothing but the Halloween doings at the Valentine Retreat Center. Big doings there. If you know of something we'd be interested."

"No, no, nothing," he replied. He did take a subscription to the paper and read the front page eagerly. In December one day on the 6th page beneath the fold, a short article announced cryptically the closing of the Valentine Retreat and Nature Center after the third disappearance, in as many years, of an elderly guest.

Mountain Top Fortress

As I passed the Red House tollbooth one day in May, there was Old Baldy, its green-covered cone standing above the rest of the hills to the south, taunting me with rumors of an ancient Indian fortress.

Old Baldy

I drove around onto Bay State Road to get closer. I parked at the North Country trailhead map. Old Baldy was plain enough on the map but as I looked uphill from this new position, it had vanished behind lower hills, gone, like a ghost.

There I was, about two in the afternoon, with no rush to get home and Old Baldy playing peek a-boo. So why don't I go for a look? Well, I'm alone, in sneakers; I haven't got a map, a compass, water, or any spare food. I'm totally unprepared, but it's not a long hike. I've got nothing else to do.

Mike had given me directions to Old Baldy and the information that old timers say there are ruins of an ancient Indian fort at its top. "You can't miss Old Baldy. As you leave on the Red House Road to Route 17, it's the peak, over on the left." He hadn't found the fort, nor had Tom or Bob or any of the younger members at that Allegany State Park Historical Society meeting,

Hook France and Roland Remington, two old-time Park hands, had been up and down it all their lives, they said.

Hook told us, "Dad used to go up there for chestnuts, 'til all the American chestnuts around here died. That's why they called it Old Baldy".

Patting his own bald dome Remington said, "You mean this?" Then added, "We went up there for school picnics. Told us, Indians used it for a lookout up and down the river. Sent smoke signals."

They hooked me. I did some research at the library and over the phone. Then I had to see for myself.

That May afternoon, I took a careful look at the trailhead map. That's Old Baldy right there. I follow this crick and just head for the highest ground. How can I miss? Then I come back down the way I go up. Right? Well, maybe.

I followed the trail a short way, then took off uphill to the southeast. Down low the meadows were lush-green, seasoned with violets and buttercups. A brigade of cattails guarded a marshy spot, which I skirted. Bees buzzed in warm sunshine. I began to sweat. I hopped the trickle in the crick, made my way through brush bordering it and broke out into tall 90-year-old forest of beech, hemlock, maple and oak.

Most of the way the forest floor was open under a dense green canopy. The way steepened. Fallen giant trees encrusted with white dinner plate fungus and garnished with immense mushrooms blocked my progress. I circled. I tried to keep the moss-covered boulders of the crick in view to my right. I lost them. My path would not be easy to follow back. So I began marking it by leaning dead branches against trees.

I thought of Hansel and Gretel leaving their breadcrumb-trail in the forest to escape the witch. The Stone Giants of the Iroquois stories came to mind; those giant warriors whose skin was so tough no arrow could penetrate it. One time the Iroquois were warned that the Stone Giants were to attack. They took refuge on a mountaintop and watched as the giants were crushed in the valley by a massive upheaval of stone. Some say that the giant rock formations at Rock City are the remains of that cataclysm.

The forest blocked my view toward that place. I sat down in the soft humus to catch my breath. A spotted two-inch newt watched me as I brushed away gnats and sweat. A chipmunk startled me as he darted along the forest highway provided him by a downed tree.

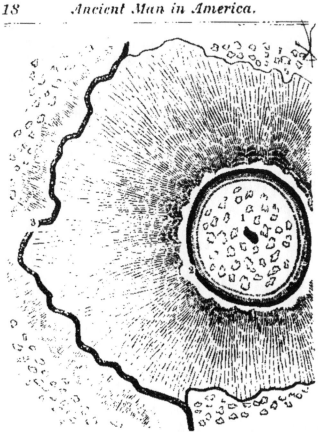

18   Ancient Man in America.

Fig. 6.—Great Fortification in the town of Red House. Figure 1, spring; 2, vallum; 3, Red House Creek.

Several miles below the Red House Creek, the remains of an ancient work can be traced. This is circular in form and about three hundred feet in diameter. Before it was disturbed the wall was four feet in height, with a ditch about six feet in

Fredrick Larkin, Ancient *Man in America*, 1880

Gogansah, the false-face maker, may have felt a similar startle when Gonusquah stepped into his view. They say

Gonusquah, the last of the Stone Giants, a man-eater, hid in the Allegany Mountains after the disaster. The giant spared Gogansah and let him go on living in the woods, carving false-faces from live trees.

A 1984 Cultural Resource Survey of Allegany State Park put me on to that story. It also comments, "The Senecas will not tell outsiders why they consider Old Baldy out of bounds" and that, "It has also been suggested that the Horned Serpent lived there rather than a Stone Giant."

Dennis Bowen, a Seneca historian said, "Senecas were never much interested in Old Baldy. Some say Horned Serpent came up out of the ground back at Rolling Thunder. That's the next big Valley in the Park off 280 after the expressway."

Dr. Robert Dean, a Seneca archaeologist said, "Sure, I been up there. Don't know what to make of them rocks. Site doesn't look like a late woodland upland village. I plan to look it over some more though." He sent me the references to Old Baldy, which he had collected: Cheney 1859, Larkin 1880, Parker 1922.*

Each of these depicts a steep 200-foot high hill with a commanding view. The hill is partially surrounded by Red House Brook and two tributaries located about one mile from the Allegany River. A two-foot deep trench and three-foot high wall make a 1,060-foot perimeter just below its top and at its center is a spring. The three writers used exactly the same numbers. Cheney and Larkin use even some of the same colorful language, as they conjure images of warriors and a fort under siege: "copious spring," "rapid streams," "deep ravines."

Larry Kilmer, the expert on the Park's 54 miles of former railroad, commented on Old Baldy in the Salamanca Republican. He details stone and mica objects found in the Salamanca area suggesting links to the ancient Mound Builders culture of the Mississippi Valley. He includes speculation about the domestication of mammoths suggested by an image on a copper relic.

Dr. Kevin Smith, the anthropologist at the Buffalo Museum of Science, discussed the ruins with me. "Yes, there were a whole string of Indian fortresses or palisaded villages stretching from Lake Erie down toward Olean. There is a well-documented one in Limestone."

I looked around me in the dense and quiet forest. It was eerie being alone there. I knew of the Native American Graves Protection and Repatriation Act of 1990, a federal law that recognized Indian rights to the sanctity of their sacred places and the remains of their ancestors. It has required museums holding Indian burial goods or remains to return them to their tribes.

I wondered, am I intruding here? Was Gonusquah concealing himself behind that giant hemlock? Was Robert Dean in that bush objecting to my amateur archeology? What false-face spirits wandered homeless here, what spirits from long dead battles?

I stirred myself and climbed higher. The pitch grew steeper. I grabbed saplings to pull me up. Then I came upon a ridge. At first it seemed only a respite in the climb. But the bit of flatness seemed to circle the peak. It was not the well-defined 5 feet of ditch and wall described by Cheney. Maybe 140 years changed that. I imagined how the ridge might have looked with a double walled palisade of three or four-inch logs worked into its earth. I followed the ridge around for several hundred feet, not always convinced that it was still there.

Blue sky and sunshine showed between tree trunks ahead. I could see the outline of a conical top. I found myself on a flat summit still heavily treed but with a clear, deer-browsed understory. The shape was oblong oriented, as best I could judge without a compass, north and south. I explored it.

Then there it was. I felt like I had discovered Machu Picchu in Buffalo's back yard. Five round, rock-walled pits set together with sides touching like a transectioned beehive. The largest was twelve by eight feet and had partially above-ground walls, three feet in height, rising in eight courses of flat stones somewhat larger than bricks. A hundred-and-fifty feet north was a less well-preserved repeat of this structure.

I took pictures. I got down in the bottom of one pit and dug in the leaves I found no sign of a spring. I remembered how Allegany's rattlesnakes like rocky places. I scrambled out saying a prayer to the Horned Serpent.

I tried a war whoop "Eeeeyahoo."

It was wonderfully disorienting, standing there alone with eons of history surrounding me and speculations whirling in my head. But that was not the only reason I wound up lost on the way down. I really should have brought along a map and a compass.

I found only the last few of my trail markers. I wound up in a deep gully leading, I feared, into the remote interior of the Park. As I mused on my best course I was hypnotized by an intricate spider web glistening as it stretched between hemlocks above me. Then suddenly, too near my face its owner, a weirdly beautiful black and orange arachnid, charged me in anger.

I departed relying on the Boy Scout theory; "Downstream leads to civilization." Finally I came out of the forested ravine in view of Red House Road but on the far side of a wide stretch of Red House Brook. Instead of swimming, I took a long walk around the flanks of Old Baldy back to my car at the North Country trailhead. I was tired, hungry, thirsty and exhilarated.

Epilogue: Robert Dean and Kevin Smith both say that Indians did not build rock structures like that. Europeans did.

Cheney and Larkin both say the fortified hill on Red House Brook is 200 feet high. Old Baldy stands 700 feet above the valley floor and has no spring, copious or otherwise. My explorations are not done.

*Cheney, T. Apoleon, 1859 Ancient Monuments in Western NY, Page 42, Larkin, Fredrick, 1880 Ancient Man in America, Page 17 Parker, Arthur C, The Archeological History of New York, Part II, Cattaraugus County Site 16, Page 498.

Audubon's Nature Pilgrimage

It's the last weekend of May. Allegany State Park's Tudor Greathouse sits above shimmering Red House Lake. Spring peepers screech their mates to wakefulness. Now, before the upper canopy of Allegany's 100 to 350-year-old forest closes in, trillium bursts joyfully into bloom. Hundreds of other wild herbs and bugs and snakes of many species and perhaps even the ghost of the vanished Allegany hellbender spring to life. What is that rustle-bumble-laughing-whisper we hear?

It's Audubon's Allegany Nature Pilgrims, of course, converging on the Park. They gather now as they have done for four decades, old folks, young folks, families with kids, natural history scientists and greenhorns. They whisper about redstarts, and gasp over jack-in-the pulpits and salamanders. They are eager to witness this annual burst of earth's energy, to teach and learn about it as they soak up the returning sun's life-giving warmth.

So what is the Allegany Nature Pilgrimage? It is a spring weekend when people, fascinated by the workings of nature, gather in Allegany State Park to celebrate and study those wonders. The Audubon Society runs it, but for a modest fee, all are welcome. In 1960 the first 80 pilgrims gathered in the Red House Administration Building. The affair has rolled on for forty years, its numbers ranging up to 1500.

In this year, 2000, the Allegany Nature Pilgrimage will be the

weekend of June 2, 3+4. For schedule and registration

information call Marcia Wagner 716-754-4231 or Audubon's

Everyone declares the Allegany Nature Pilgrimage to be O. Gilbert "Gib" Burgeson's baby. Gib had been to the Spring Wildflower Pilgrimage sponsored by the University of Tennessee in Great Smoky Mountain National Park. He came back saying, "We have got to do that in Allegany." In 1959 he persuaded his own club, Jamestown Audubon, plus three Buffalo Societies: Audubon, Ornithological and the Museum of Science to set up a committee that would run an Allegany Nature Pilgrimage. Since then, Rochester and Presque Isle Audubon and the Park itself have joined in the sponsorship. Buffalo Ornithological has dropped out.

Gib, whose specialty was the potted wildflower display, taught at 37 Pilgrimages. Harold Stock, a Pilgrimage organizing committee member, describes Gib:

"I went on a nature walk led by a little man who wore a little pork-pie hat, and a warm smile that could turn any gray day into a sunny warm experience. I can still hear him say, 'Let me take you into my classroom,' as he pushed a bushy branch back that revealed an afternoon of natural wonders."

Gib's perfect attendance record was interrupted when he died on his 100th birthday in 1997.

Many families have come for years. Jane and Harold Stock have been here as a couple for 25 years, her family for 30. They are into four generations. Jane's mother was the traditional packer for the family. She loaded the car with everything from bathing suits to galoshes. They kidded her about all the junk she brought but never objected to the comfortable home she could make of most any barren Allegany cabin.

The Stocks used to favor Congdon Trail, until one year Jane and her daughter came down a day early. They put out the lights in that ancient cabin and went to bed. Suddenly they were beset by flying dragons with huge luminescent eyes. The ladies felt grasping, clawed feet through their bed covers as the creatures launched themselves from rafters and walls to light on them in their beds. They fled screaming into the dark, slamming the cabin door behind them.

Outside in pajamas and slippers they realized that the keys to their car and the cabin were locked inside the cabin. Early in the morning, after sitting up in the car all night, they hiked to the Administration Building. The stone bridge on Red House creek was washed out that year so on the way they ran a gauntlet of mouthy, whistling construction workers.

A maintenance supervisor explained the monsters. He had cut down a tree containing a nest of flying squirrels, behind their cabin.

Corel "Corky" Belknap is another old standby whose name was mentioned over and over as I probed the history of the

Allegany Pilgrimage. She is a 78-year-old retired teacher and was a good buddy of Gib Burgeson's. Corky admits that, though she helped plan it and has been to all the rest of them, she missed the first pilgrimage.

According to Frances Rew, a Science Museum birding instructor, she and Corky were both members of the original Pilgrimage organizing committee. "We had the first meeting in the Buffalo Museum of Science," Frances said. "That year we only met the once. We handled the rest all by phone. We tried to make the Pilgrimage something serious, like the Buffalo Museum's Allegany School of Natural History back in the thirties, but it turned into a picnic in the Park. I only stuck with it a few years. I'm more active with the Ornithological Society now." She added ironically, "Gib missed that first committee meeting. He was off on a trip to Florida."

Corky remained a member of the committee for many years but says, "Now I leave the chores to the younger ones. I guess we found a system that works no matter how many people come and we just kept using it." To back that up Corky sent me documentation: "The Constitution of the Allegany Nature Pilgrimage Committee" and "The Committee Job Descriptions and Timetable." They spell out exactly how to run a Pilgrimage.

From the Pilgrim's point of view, here is how it works. By phone, you book a cabin or campsite reservation with the Park. You register at Camp Allegany on the Red House side of the Park and there you receive a list of classes and events. Classes are assigned meeting places on the road circling Red House Lake. A sign is posted at each spot. You pick what interests you and at the assigned time you join your group at the lake.

Last year the list of field trips and classes included:

Beginning and Advanced Birding, Blowdown Birding, Bike Hikes, Backpacking, Reptiles and Amphibians, Pond Life, Basic or Advanced Tracking, Park Geology and History, Wildflowers, Plant and Tree Lore, Exploration Walks, Babes in the Woods, Nature Relaxation, Splash Hike, Nature Photography, 3 or 5 Mile Hike, Ecology, Naturally Safe, Attracting Wildlife, Hikes to Black Snake Mountain, Allenburg Bog, and All Day Birding, Bug Light at Night, Moon Walks, Astronomy............ Plus 17 listed under "And much much much more."

Registration was in a room of the conference building at Camp Allegany. In the next room were Dick Christensen's ambitious wildflower display and Lincoln Nutting's dazzling wildflower photographs. Behind that building was the circus tent where the chicken barbecue was served and evening programs were held. That evening Keith Bildstein showed slides of the 20,000 hawks that migrate over Hawk Mountain, Pennsylvania each year. The next night Bill Thompson, Birdwatcher Digest Editor, pitched his book, "Birdwatching For Dummies."

Last summer, I picked a nature hike up Black Snake Mountain led by Wayne Gall. I think I found him as engaging as Harold Stock found Gib Burgeson. Wayne is probably twice as big as Gib but has the same friendly, enthusiastic manner. He knew personally, and wanted to introduce each of us to, every plant, tree, bird and bug on the mountain.

Besides Black Snake and the evening programs, I did Geology of the Park and a beaver pond hike. The history session, I had considered, was canceled, so I took a friend on a walk to Allegany's "Little Ireland," near Thunder Rock, off the Limestone Road.

Beaver lodge field trip

Thunder Rock Trip

The people and the old reliable Pilgrimage format provided plenty of other action. The sun was shining. People were laughing, eating, catching up with old friends and spotting birds. Kids were chasing each other, looking under rocks for snakes, splashing about and having a good time.

A big event Saturday evening is the roll call of birds seen that day. Harold Stock implied that sometimes there appears to be a bit of imagination or exaggeration in play with regard to rare birds identified. He recalls once, the fellow that supervised the bird roll call placed a stuffed chicken in a tree near the big tent. "For a time he really had them going," Harold said. "They were calling it some kind of a weird hawk or a buzzard."

For those not ready for bed after the evening program on Saturday there is the Owl Prowl. I joined one in the pitch black on the back road into Camp 12. Frances Rew had raved about seeing three species of owl on one such an expedition: barred, horned and screech. A Buffalo News article on the 1966 Pilgrimage quotes biology professor Edward Seeber on an owl prowl calling in owls with his hooting, "Ho-ho-ho-ho-o-o-o-o. What you're saying is: 'I'm taking over this territory, Mr. Owl, and you better get out of here.'" He explained if things go right then the local owner-owl comes down to fight. "That is when the excitement is greatest for the owl howlers, when they turn on their flashlights and see Mr. Owl there, sometimes not more than 15 feet away, blinking and ruffling his feathers and wishing someone would turn the lights out and leave him alone."

I've been on three late-night, cool, dampish owl prowls now and have as yet to hear, or see, owl one. However, on the drive back to my cabin, over in Quaker, I saw 1 raccoon, 2 foxes, 5 porcupines and 13 deer.

Almost everyone I spoke to painted the Pilgrimage in idyllic tones, at first. But I asked for problems. Corky Belknap searched reluctantly, "When they started taking reservations in California, instead of here, that was a problem. Two families would wind up with reservations for the same cabin. I'd have to march down there and straighten it out. Attendance dropped then, too."

I pressed her, "Anything else?"

"Well, you know we moved out of the Administration Building and into the old Red House Town Hall, below the dam. Pretty soon we were jammed in there. We moved to a circus tent opposite the Red House swimming beach. That was fine, except for the dance hall. In the 40's we used to love to come over from Jamestown for the dances. But this was Rock and Roll time. The noise from those bands drowned out our evening programs and there were a lot of people drinking and hanging around. We solved that by talking to the Park Administration and by hiring off-duty police."

"We got big enough for a while that we filled up most of the Park. The Police loved us because it was one weekend when they could expect peace and quiet. Maintenance loved us, too, because we picked up trash. Now, the Museum of Science has given over Camp Allegany to us for the weekend. We were kind of afraid that we would be away from everything back over in there but it has worked out just fine."

I pressed on, "I spoke on the phone to a volunteer at one of the Audubon offices. She said something about a scandal?"

"Oh, you mean the time the treasury was embezzled?"

Most of the people I spoke to got around to that incident. It is probably sufficient to say about it that the Pilgrimage was vital enough to survive even that kind of a several-thousand-dollar bump-in-the-road.

For controversy, I did not have to press Blake Reeves, a long time member of Audubon and an avid birder and botanist. He asked me, immediately, "Are you writing an article or a puff piece?"

I stumbled. He went on, "I am in the Park at the time of the Pilgrimage. There is a fantastic display of forest herbs then but I don't attend any of the doings anymore. There has been a split. There is no longer truly an interest in organisms and their community. Many of the programs have no natural history connection at all. We had hoped that we would have a renewal of the Allegany School of Natural History. Now it's just recreation."

Blake, chuckling at the low blow he was delivering said, "Look at last year's main speaking attraction, 'Birding for Dummies.'"

"What would you like to see done differently?" I asked.

"An advanced course in birding. Some of those people with excellent field skills to distinguish immature sparrows from one another or female warblers. Experts in the really hard fields: mosses and lichens and more difficult areas of botany. This Allegany Pilgrimage was modeled after the Wildflower Pilgrimage in the Smokies. Those folks have a terrific list of courses. They do dream natural history." Blake tailed of with a chuckle, "Talk to

Dick Christensen. He's a good naturalist and a good friend of mine but he sees it differently."

Gib Burgeson was also a critic according to a Buffalo Courier article in 1981. "'It's getting out of hand,' he says with distaste: 'Now, they've added hiking and backpacking and jogging. There's no place for them. People are going through the woods without learning anything about nature.'"

When I raised Blake's objections with Peg and Dick Christensen, Peg cracked, "Nothing is ever scientific enough for Blake."

Dick said, "Seventeen or eighteen years ago I had the job of organizing the class leaders. I had to face the quandary: The kids want to throw stones and other folks want to study stuff like ambient oxygen levels. So we had separate kid and family events. We'd have something for everyone, like the astronomers setting up telescopes to look at different phases of the moon. Then we'd have basic birding and insect trips and we'd have advanced levels of those subjects."

Dick shrugged, "But there were always some leaders that came late or didn't show up." With a shrug of relief he said, "I helped Gib with the wildflower display till he couldn't do it anymore. For ten years now that's been my job."

Dick and Peg bring a van load of labeled wildflowers for display in pots, at least 50 of them: wild geraniums, hepatica, buttercups, violets, jack-in-the-pulpits, pink ladyslipper and many kinds of ferns: marsh, New York, lady and so on, beyond my ability to record. Peg said, "People put their names in the pots, to reserve the plants, to take home. Someone always comes back complaining, 'They took my hepatica.'"

"It's a good weekend for kids," said Dick. "The bird bander sets up yards of fine net to snare small birds. They put tiny bands on their legs to study migratory patterns. You get to see birds up close. One bander rocks a bird to sleep in his hands, like magic, and puts it on a kid's head, till it wakes up and flies off. The kids love that."

Peg chimed in, "Wayne Gall is a good example of a kid catching the bug down there. He started coming with his mother as a little kid. Now, he is the entomologist at the Museum and he leads general nature trips on the Pilgrimage."

After the 26th Pilgrimage, Buffalo News Nature Columnist and Pilgrimage nature trip leader, Dave Bigelow, wrote of his own favorite teaching spot, a mile south of Red House:

"---we have always found a male ruby-throated hummingbird perched on a dead snag high over the trail that enters the forest beyond the willows.--- 'There he is!' a woman cried, turning her binoculars toward the one dead branch of the canopy. I followed her gaze and soon recognized the fiery red flashes of its crimson gorget.

Gerry Rising admits, in his Buffalo News nature column, that the 1993 Pilgrimage was his first, though he had been a long time hiker in the Park. Gerry touched on the controversy then raging over logging in the Park, a "sour note" that divided the Park staff from the members of Audubon. "It is sad to find these two groups, whose goals are so nearly aligned, so far apart on this admittedly divisive issue."

Then Gerry brings us all, staff and pilgrims, back together with this scene, "Dennis Wilson, the Jamestown forester, ---is identifying witchhazel for us when his daughter's sharp eyes pick out a fawn curled at its base, the young deer's white spots and soft brown, blending in perfectly with the forest floor. It lies so still that only the slight motion of its breathing assures us that it is alive."

Before I quit, I have got to tell you the Stock family's bear story. Jane Stock and one of her girlfriend birders, two days into a busy Pilgrimage had an irresistible appetite for pizza from a certain pizzeria in Bradford. They hopped in a car and sped to town. Returning with the delicious fragrance of oregano and pepperoni exhuding from the car, Jane thought she saw a Pileated woodpecker flash through the trees. The two of them piled out of the car, binoculars in hand, to charge into the woods. They returned to find a bear sitting on the trunk of their car, licking his chops and sniffing for a way in.

The turbulent stew of families and individuals, of teachers and students, of eager beavers and flower children that is the Allegany Nature Pilgrimage has established an impressive record. Their rite of spring has persisted for forty years. It entertains. It teaches knowledge of and respect for the natural environment. It is amazingly well attended and it continues despite a considerable share of controversy.

Among these varied people, two exemplary types stand out. The old folks with dreams like Gib Burgeson and Corky Belknap and kids growing up like Dennis Wilson's sharp-eyed daughter and Wayne Gall, the bug wizard, all eager to pass along what they were inspired to learn here in Allegany.

Muzzle Loading
Rendezvous, Wolf Run

Letter to the Buffalo News
August 24, 1997, 10:30pm

I saw the Buffalo News article on the National Muzzle Loading Rifle Association's Rendezvous at Wolf Run in Allegany State Park. Owning an antique rifle I sometimes like to fantasize about being a mountain man in the old days. So I went down for a look

Muzzle Loader Rifle Rendezvous, Allegany 1997

I had not thought about how many people 3500 is and what they could do to 50 acres of wilderness. Imagine for a moment the

Erie County Fair held in a swamp, or Woodstock on the way to becoming the Confederate prison at Andersonville. You're getting close. Imagine a hoard of congenial, well-meaning locusts intent on having a good time descending on a meadow in four-wheel drive vehicles, while it's raining.

Cars were parked on both sides of Highway 280 and both sides of Wolf Run Road for the 2.5 miles of pavement until the mud road that runs through the encampment. There the cars spilled out to fill a third of the fifty acres of mowed-down prime wildlife habitat which park officials had prepared for the campers. The rest of those acres swarmed with interestingly clad people, their primitive tents and their two hundred port-a-potties. Their thousand or so damp smoldering fires filled the air with smoke. Their vehicles filled the meadows with ruts; tractors fought to extract the more deeply buried ones and a road scraper tried to turn wilderness into thoroughfare for them.

Two rifle ranges filled the woods with blam, blam, blam and black powder smoke. The construction of horse corrals made of 3 to 4 inch diameter trees has given at least one corner of the regenerating forest there a considerable setback.

Rifle Range

I met a friend slogging through the mud. We each shook our heads. He said, ''This used to be such a wonderful place.''

I don't know who to feel the sorriest for, those poor Muzzle Loader folks who came from all over the US to spoil our park in mud, the frightened rattlesnakes Wolf Run is noted for or us, the people who try to use the Park gently.

Can this mess possibly be worth the $13,000 the Park is supposed to get for it? I don't think so.

"Cold and Rainy Allegany," go ahead. Do your thing.

118

Muzzle Loader Encampment
and
Sierra

October 28 1997
Resolution regarding:

The National Muzzle Loader Rifle Association Primitive Encampment held in Allegany State Park during August of 1997. This is to advise the Allegany State Park Management and New York State OPRHP that in our opinion the decision to permit the National Muzzle Loader Rifle Association Primitive Encampment at Wolf Run was an error. Sierra Club visited the Wolf Run site before, during and after the encampment.

The two to three thousand campers who crowded into those 36 acres for a week have left the meadow badly scarred with stumps, muddy ruts, fire pits and trampled vegetation. Some campers constructed fencing for horses and wooden tent walls using local materials. There still stands a primitive picnic table and a large stone-lined barbecue pit. The several rifle ranges that we found active during our visit could not help but leave permanent traces in the woods.

The culverted roads installed by the Park are the most massive and long-lasting change to the character of the place. They turn that recovering meadow into an inefficient mass-campsite and parking lot.

Primitive camping, in the usual sense, is done in small numbers and in such a way as to leave little or no imprint on the land. This encampment was a tent city of no small proportion. There is no way such a city can be placed in a meadow or woods without severely impacting the resource.

Sierra is in sympathy with the intent of the Muzzle Loader organization to create and enjoy a frontier experience. We share many of their sentiments about the outdoors and times gone by but that style of camping is destructive to a natural setting. It should be held in a commercial place willing to make the sacrifice, not in a public park trying to preserve natural habitat.

Sierra believes not only that the decision to allow the encampment was ill-advised but that some of its results were, in fact, illegal. We cite Title 9 of The New York State Rules and Regulations, Volume a3, Section 408.1. "Injury to property: No Person shall make an excavation or injure, destroy, deface, remove, fill in, tamper with or cut any real or personal property, tree or other plant life, and no person shall erect or maintain any structure except as otherwise provided in this subchapter."

Certainly the Park's expansion of "camping facilities" in this radical way departs from the spirit of negotiation with which OPRHP has approached the upcoming Allegany State Park Master Plan.

Sierra urges OPRHP and the Allegany State Park Administration to rule out any further use of the Park for such, to it, inappropriate events.

Civilian Conservation Corps
Reunion 1997
An ORAL HISTORY

Light rain was falling and it was cool that day in mid May when I pulled into Camp Turner over in Quaker Run for the Civilian Conservation Corps reunion. But the weather had not dampened the spirits of about forty CCC veterans and their wives congregated there already. These grizzled pioneers, in their late seventies, had been in the Park in all kinds of weather and before there were modern buildings like those at Camp Turner.

They talked, laughed and exchanged tall tales, as they soaked up coffee and doughnuts. I was late and I was supposed to be getting those stories down on tape. It took me three tape recorders and a trip back to Red House before I found one that the Park secretary would let me take.

The C's were full of stories. Some of them were shy and had to be coaxed, some so primed that I had to turn them off to work anyone else in. All five of the men I recorded had been in the CCC in the late thirties, from age 17 or 18 to 19 or 20. Three of them served in Allegany State Park and two out West. They all remembered the terrible conditions of the Depression. There were no jobs, no money and not much to eat. They were grateful for the cash they earned in the Corps that fed their families while they were away.

Three of the five went into military service immediately after the CCC and served as non-commissioned officers in WWII. "We knew how to get along in a camp. How to make up a bunk. Our sergeant brought a silver dollar to inspection. If it didn't bounce when he tossed it on the bunk it was KP for you."

They all spoke well of President Roosevelt, they called him FDR, and credited him with inventing the CCC.

Arthur was a husky, well-spoken man in a green satin CCC baseball jacket and cap. He had shaken hands with FDR while on duty with the CCC. The day before this reunion he had been to the dedication of the FDR monument in Washington. "He was a great man," Arthur said.

Arthur did his CCC service in Colorado, building fences between sheepherders and cattlemen. "They didn't much like us out there, at first. But then they warmed up. After while they were bringing horses out to us to ride for fun."

Arthur's favorite story was about beans. "We had a Commanding Officer who was Mexican and he liked beans. He fed us beans all the time. I never seen so many different kind of beans, some you soak overnight, some for two days or even a week.

I was out working one day and when I came back everyone was sitting down. They wouldn't work. So I sat down, too. It was a strike about them beans. Eventually it went to court and we won. The food got very good after that."

Arthur was proud of not drinking or gambling while he was in the CCC. As a result he was able to save additional money to send home. "We got 30 dollars a day," he said looking at me for a response.

I said, "Yeah, but just once a month. My uncle told me that one."

"You stole my punch line," he said. "We'd get $5 and $25 would get sent home to our folks."

"Some of us used to loan-out money to the guys who spent all of theirs. We had regular rates: Borrow $1 for a week and pay back $1.25, then $1.50 for two weeks and $1.75 for three. We had a good Captain. The guys who loaned-out money sat at a table and right after the others got paid, he'd say, `You owe anything you go right over there to the table and pay it off.'"

Christopher had a different attitude about loaning money at exorbitant rates. He was a tall, vigorous man who stooped a little. He wore a homemade overseas cap with CCC in gold braid sewed on one side.

I asked if he ever ran into any trouble in the CCCs.

"Trouble? We got rid of trouble as soon as we saw any. There were loan sharks who collected 25% a week when they loaned money. We got rid of them. There were card sharps with decks marked on the edge and dice loaded with weights so they'd always come up seven or eleven. I took them dice away and won back thirty dollars off the cheaters and paid it back to the losers. Then I burned the dice and showed them the weights."

Fortunately Arthur and Christopher did not get into the conversation at the same time or there might have been fireworks.

Christopher was an eager talker. "I worked on the surveying crew," he said. "We laid out Ryan trail. Those were really nice cabins." He specified the wood types used in the floors, walls, roofs and for paneling. I finished the school house for them over near the Red House entrance where the sawmill is now. I piled up stones all winter and they went in to building the stone observation tower.

I was the assistant librarian in the school and a champion fisherman out of Red House Lake. Our barracks won all the trophies for baseball and volley ball."

He too had a "bean" story. "You go walking in the barracks at night and there was an awful racket. But when you hear the big guns go off you want to keep on going or open the windows up wide." Here he held his nose and waved his right arm as if airing out a room. "Too many beans they fed us."

Christopher told a curious story about a dog. "I was in bed and this little black poodle jumped up and laid on my feet and came up and licked my face. He had some bristly black hair stuck on him. He'd come and spend some time with me and then disappear. I followed him to a bear cave and found him playing with two bear cubs and the mother bear watching them. Once when we were in formation he showed up. The Captain shouted `Whose dog is that?' The poodle jumped up on a lady visitor. She looked at his collar and said, `I guess he's mine. Sometimes he goes wild for awhile.'"

Christopher believed the CCC should be revived. "But this time with men and women. And you know what they should do? Build a coastal sea wall of steel to protect the barrier islands."

I agreed with him that a modern CCC might be a good idea and persuaded him we should take a break for lunch.

After a break for a turkey dinner and speeches, I looked for more stories. Bill was standing near my station but he wouldn't talk to me at all, on tape. I turned off the machine and asked him a few questions. He got going, his buddy chipped in, their two wives joined the conversation and then a third couple, friends of theirs, started talking. In the middle of this, I turned my machine on, in such a way that everyone could see that they were being recorded. They were rolling so well that not even Bill objected.

CCC stone observation tower 2002

Ryan Trail

Wilbur was the serious one and Bill went for laughs. He teased me, "Is that the only rat you got?" as a mouse, that had been hanging around me all day, ran out from under my chair.

I answered without a flinch, "That's my last one so you can't have him."

Bill and Wilbur were both from a nearby town and the CCC assigned them to work in Allegany State Park. Bill drove a truck and learned forestry. Wilbur built "walking trails" and roads. Both helped to put up the Quaker Run fire tower.

I asked them, "How was the food?"

Wilbur said, "Oh, it was good...and plenty of it.

Bill said, "Yeah, it was pretty good, considering you didn't get much to eat at home those days.

"Did you get deer or bear meat from the Park?" I asked.

"No, we didn't get none of that, more likely luncheon meat, Bill answered."

I asked the group what they did for fun and Bill's wife said "Probably looked for girls." They all laughed.

I asked "Were there CCC dances?"

Someone said "Oh sure."

Bill's wife said, "Maybe there was but he must have taken someone else. I was too young. Only 14 when we met. He was hitchhiking home and my brother picked him up in his truck. We never went anywhere except with my mother. We were married when I was sixteen."

Mike's wife said, "I was pregnant when Mike went off to Colorado."

I said something to Mike like, "That must have been tough, going off then."

He said, "Well, my Dad died. He was only 41. My brother and I wanted to run the farm but my mother wouldn't have it. I went to work in a basket factory and then in a juice factory but they didn't pay nothing."

"So you went into the CCC for the money?" I asked. I was surprised to see him choke up.

His wife said to him, consolingly, "Now, don't get into

that."

Mike blurted out, "She got shafted. She was supposed to get half the allotment."

"But your mother got the whole thing?" I asked.

"That's right. Her Dad was a good guy though and he took good care of her."

Mike and his wife have had four more kids after that one and are very proud of them.

Almost everyone had stories about bears raiding the garbage near camp but the only one who had met a rattlesnake was Bill's wife. "I was hiking up on Beehunter with the kids and there was a big old rattler," she said.

The last story I heard came from Mike. "There was this short, real muscular tough guy whose brother was a heavyweight boxer. He was always pushing people around. One day he was picking on this tall lanky kid. They called him Red because of his hair. The kid whirled around and landed a good one right on this guy's jaw, so he went down. The kid said, `I just saw red.' Anyway, they shook hands and were best buddies after that."

The group left to tour the Quaker Museum. I went along to turn my precious tape over to Mike Miecznikowski. I took Mike's soul in pawn for that tiny irreplaceable repository of American history. He promised to try to persuade the chief Park secretary to transcribe it.

*(The quotations I used in this account are condensed Approximations. I changed the names of participants. The Allegany State Park Historical Society has the complete tape.)

Uncle Bernard Beahan's
CCC Scrap Book

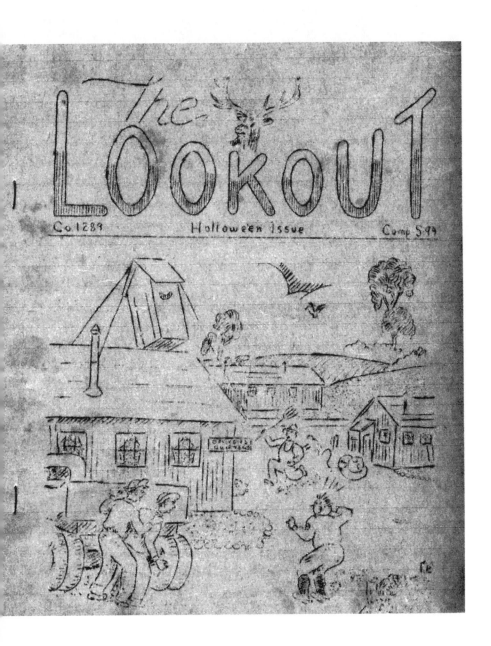

128

Diary of Rita B. Lackey's brother who served in the CCC's in 1935

DIARY OF A 3-C PEAVIE

April 30- Rained nearly all day so we got a day of rest, but
it will be made up by work on Saturday. The boys were rather
restless. A few new fellows came in today and the veterans
had quite a bit of fun initiating them. We got paid at
about 3:30 P.M. and most of the men started spending their
moneyu immediately. My second day as table waiter.

May 4- Scholiel was on a rampage today. He sent Paul Baur
back to camp for not [lanting the trees the correct distance
apart. Then he started "riding" me. He was just looking for
an excuse to send me in. But I wouldn't give him any
satisfaction. I felt like giving him a cute talk; but I
thought discretion was the better part of valor.

May 5- Missed mass today. Had to work in the kitchen from
9;30 till a little after 3 PM. My last day as table waiter
for this "hitch". Raining again.

May 6- Quite cloudy. Schofield is still after me. He
changed me from mattock to pail. He tried to awfully hard to
get me to refuse to work but I didn't pay any attention to
his bulldozing tactics.

May 7- Raining all day. No work detail. A few of the
fellows were shooting crap mosly all day. Some of them
"checked out" in the afternoon. Physical inspection in A.M.
'Shoot the Six' nickel open nickel he lights " filled the
barrack air waves the better part of the day. One fellow in
our barracks is trying to land a repointorial position on the
Syracuse Journal (Paul Baur).

May 8- Beautiful, warm day. Last night our leader got
knocked out by one of the convoy drivers. Ball _ying
tonight. I don't like to hear the fellows "shooting the
bull" all the time. It gets rather tiresome, listening to
all the cuss words and foul imprecations. Sounds like a
cross between Billingsgate and stevedore's convention. At
present there are only 7 fellows in my barracks and two of
them are due to "check out"in a few minutes. Some are
playing ball others have gone to Harrisville and still to
the various surrounding villages and cities.

May 9- Warm, sun shiny day. Planted spruce, white pine, and
balsam today. About a week more of tree planting.

May 10- I got a Fri.night pass left camp after late chow;
arrived in _____ at 2 minutes of six rode down on the
bread truck. Seemed pretty good to see the hometown again.
Saw private Von____.

Saturday, May 11- Dr. Lashur filled two teeth for me today.
He plans to fill the rest of them next Saturday.

8

Snake Eyes

(I spun this tale, of the CCC in Allegany State Park, out of newspaper clippings and conversations with CCC veterans from Allegany, garnished with material from my uncle and my father-in-law both of whom served in the CCC, but upstate and out west.)

"You chicken-hearted, lily-livered, country-punk, what on God's green earth am I supposed to do about it?" yelled CCC Platoon Leader Edward Christian Kelly that summer day in the late thirties. Two men confronted one another in a bunkhouse-office at Camp 51 where Civilian Conservation Corps Company 249 was quartered. Camp 51's Spartan buildings stood near the Red House saw mill on ASP2 amid Allegany State Park's great hills and green forests.

"But ah, Kelly---my, my mother---didn't get her check," Nineteen-year-old Civilian Conservation Corps Enrollee, Alton "Bunion" Burroughs, said as he pressed on into Kelly's office.

Bunion could handle an axe better than any man in Company 249 but he was as raw and country-green as they come. In camp he was Paul Bunion, PB or just Bunion. For a CCC enrollee, he was big, five-foot-eleven, rangy-to-skinny, like most of them but his shoulders and arms were those of a lumberjack. When upset or amused he often held his head over to the right. His hair was black. Dark smudges underlay his brown eyes and premature grooves lined his face. In better times that face had broken, easily, into a grin.

Platoon Leader Kelly had made it clear to all comers that his life here in Allegany State Park was a miserable imbalance of duty to the Corps in the person of Company CO, Captain Mienecke, versus wet-nursing what he described as a mob of half-civilized, half-starved, Bolshevik morons, the six-month CCC enrollees. Kelly tightened the muscles of his jaw and pointedly fixed his unblinking blue eyes, not on Bunion, but out of the window beyond him, to the center of the parade ground. Captain Mienecke's ten and twelve-year-old daughters played there at the stone water fountain built by the Company. Then he shifted his piercing gaze to the younger man and hissed, "You only been here three weeks, Bunion. What do you expect?"

CCC-built cabin on service road below Red House Dam

Kelly referred to his Army service in the Philippine war as "a piece of coconut-cake." He implied to the other platoon leaders that an enterprising NCO there could run his show and put something nice aside for himself. "The Army lets a Sergeant run a platoon," he often said. "In the CCC you can't put a nickel aside and they got you running a goddamn kindygarden."

And now Bunion crowded into his narrow space insisting, "I got to be taking care of my people. Those papers, something must of---" Bunion broke off as he glimpsed a Colt 45 automatic pistol in the desk drawer that Kelly, after drawing deeply on his Lucky Strike, had slammed shut.

"For rattlers and any other kind of snake-in-the-grass," Kelly said. The Company's project that summer was to build a massive stone observation tower and a road leading to it at the Park Summit. During construction they had disturbed a nest of timber rattlers. Nobody had been bitten but Captain Mienecke ordered the Company to wear canvas puttees and keep their eyes open.

Nodding toward the drawer Kelly added, "Army designed that baby for the Philippines. One of them Hucks come running at you swinging a machete, hit him anywhere and you put him down."

Bunion saw that Kelly was trying to intimidate him. He did not back down. He had grown up on a tiny farm at the edge of Northern New York State's lumber woods where his family scraped out a living at millwork or lumber jobbing to supplement income from their hard-scrabble farm. Work had dried up and Bunion was in the CCC for money to feed the family. So he was not easily put aside on money matters. "My folks are livin' on roots and rabbits. Country up there is goin' bare."

"Bunion, lesson number one here is, learn to take care of Numero Uno. Your mommy and daddy took care of themselves before you came along. They can take care of themselves now."

"You tell me, what they are going to eat."

"You get thirty dollars a day, once a month---on pay day, and the government will send twenty-two of that to your old lady."

"Kelly, Mother spent our last twenty-five cent for bakin' flour on Thursday, week."

"Why don't she get herself on relief?"

"Pa got back on at the mill."

"So?"

"They stopped the relief. Now he's off sick."

Bubbles, as Enrollee Herbert Gortz was known, crowded into the narrow office. Round-faced nineteen-year-old Bubbles, wearing general issue wire spectacles and youthful complexion problems, was Bunion's closest friend, in camp.

"Bunion, quit your belly-aching, things are tough all over," he said winking at Kelly.

Bunion turned on Bubbles forcing him into the partition, "I got to go home, unless I get hold of some cash."

"Don't look at me. I ain't no Rockefeller" said Bubbles.

"I didn't mean, for you---"

Kelly broke in, "Bunion, you signed on for six months. Get used to it. Now, I got business."

"You got my business." Bunion protested spinning around at Kelly.

"Here, here's a dollar. Pay me back, pay day," Kelly reached into his wallet, pulled out a wrinkled greenback and jammed it into Bunion's uniform shirt pocket.

"But Kelly---," Bunion protested.

Bubbles pushed his way passed Bunion, "Crying-out-loud, give someone else a chance. Kelly, I need a pass Saturday. My girl ain't right. She---"

"Yeah, yeah, don't tell me about it. And fill out the whole God damn chit, this time, okay?"

Bunion remained standing in the doorway. He hung his head even more to the right as if he were looking at his problem from all possible angles, "Kelly, I want to see the Captain. I appreciate the buck but it won't do."

"Permission denied, Enrollee."

"I want to see the Captain!"

"Mienecke doesn't want to be bothered with this kind of stuff. Now get out of here." Kelly raked his skinny fingers through his red hair, ground out the butt of his Lucky Strike in the rust of a Simon Pure Beer ashtray, rose up out of his chair swelling toward his full pugnacious five-foot six and drilled those blue eyes through Bunion.

Bunion hesitated.

Kelly growled, "Enrollee Gortz, escort this man back to his bunk immediately."

"Hey, why me? I don't know this guy from Adam."

"Bubbles, you keep this dumb hick son-of-a-bitch out of my hair or else."

"Else what?"

"You want that pass, Bubbles? Show me how good of a nurse maid you are."

"Could you at least call me Herby? Come on Bunion, let's get a beer."

Bubbles' father had been machine-gunned to death by the Coast Guard on the Niagara River during a bootlegging operation. So Bubbles and five of his siblings went to the German Roman Catholic Orphanage in Buffalo. It was five years before his mother saved enough from her waitressing at the Club 440, a speakeasy, to reunite them. In those five years Bubbles had the time to learn most of the angles necessary to survive in an institution, be it an orphanage, the Army or the CCC.

Bunion shuffled into the main section of the bunk room with Bubbles urging from behind. As always, except for a few days early in August, it was cool and damp in the Park. A wood fire was burning in the pot-bellied barracks stove and young men sat on wooden benches around it digesting supper, smoking, reading and talking of home.

"I don't want a beer," said Bunion.

"I want one. Maybe we can shoot some craps with Kelly's buck over at the canteen and run it up into some dough."

A kid said, "Bunion, tell us one of them yarns like those uncles of yours, one loaned the other a gold watch and chain."

Bunion waved him off, "Got things on my mind."

Bubbles took up his counselor-in-training stance, "You heard what Kelly said, Bunion. You got to give up on that complaining deal. Your folks'll get by. You---"

"You, what were you doin'? Tellin' him you don't know me from Adam. How come you didn't back me up?"

"You don't know how to act. You want me to get screwed out of my pass?"

"I been putting up with you snoring next to me for three weeks."

"I can't help it. I got sinus," Bubbles said.

"That time you let the axe go fly. Over to Vet's camp, on the Quaker side, was that sinus?" asked Bunion raising his eyebrows. "You almost killed that guy."

"Accidents happen."

"I kept that big I-talian stone cutter from killing you, like he should of."

"Okay, okay I just meant it's not fair for Kelly to hold up my pass 'cause you feel responsible for supporting your whole damn family."

"It's not up to you."

"He put me in charge of you. Look, after this week-end, just go home."

"That's what I ought to do," Bunion said standing up and starting to pace.

"Go on ahead."

"Won't they---?" he starts to ask as he stops abruptly turning back to Bubbles.

"What do they care? Think they're going to waste a G-man looking for a dumb hick like you?"

"They shoot you," said Bunion.

"For deserting the CCC? Are you nuts?"

"No?"

"No. They don't shoot you. I don't even think they're allowed to have guns around here. My first idea was, join up, get the uniform, maybe a new pair of specs and, as soon as nobody's looking, head for the wide open spaces," said Bubbles with a grin.

"It ain't legal."

"You could get 20 bucks easy for the boots and stuff."

"Why'd you stay?"

"I met you and fell in love. You dumb hick."

A couple of the others around the stove looked up and grinned. "Bubbles found a home in the Corps," said someone. The kid who had aske for a yarn said, "Bubbles, you never had it so good."

Bubbles turned on the kid. "Look, I'm going to ask you nice, one more time, don't call me Bubbles. My name is Herbert. Call me Herby, okay?"

The kid persisted, "Where did you get that name, Bubbles?"

As Bubbles leaned toward him, Bunion stepped between them, "You mean I could just leave and that would be the end of it?"

"Lots of guys do it. Get a little homesick and---But don't think about it till after my pass, okay?"

"I ain't homesick."

"Yeah and my girl ain't knocked up."

"I wish I lived as close here as you do so I could hitch home on a pass."

Bubbles reached for Bunion's shirt pocket, "Give me the buck. Let me show you how to make some money."

Bunion turned away fending him off and took the dollar out smoothing it across his right palm with his left hand. "Are you really any good at shooting crap?"

140

"Listen, I know everything there is to know about making money including shooting dice. Didn't I corner this KP job where all you suckers have to kick in twenty-five cents a month for us poor slobs to wait on you?"

"Myself, I'druther be in the woods anytime than swamping out grease buckets," said Bunion.

"That's why you people are poor and you're always gonna be poor."

"We ain't poor, just can't find no work. The damn Depression."

"If you'd let me manage you boxing, you could be a rich man. That day over in Quaker, the way you put down that stone cutter from Vet's Camp, one right-cross that was sheer beauty."

"My mother don't believe prize fighting is right. Take the buck. See what you can do."

"Goody, goody. We don't need a note from your old ma to go gambling now, do we?" Bubbles laughed, elbowed Bunion, snatched the dollar and headed for the door.

Outdoors, the roar of a shiny deep-blue two-year-old Reo Flying Cloud Sedan brought the two young men up short, as they entered the parade ground in the fading afternoon sunlight. At the wheel, Captain Mienecke straightened up and gave them a wave. Mrs. Mienecke nodded and smiled as the Captain guided the car passed them toward its new home in the camp barn.

The Mienecke children, Sarah and Alice, aged twelve and ten called, "Hi Bubbles. Hi Bunion," waving from the back seat window as the vehicle pulled away towards the family's modest quarters. The children knew the two enrollees because Bubbles, in his full-time kitchen job, had access to all the food he wanted. When they came to play at the stone water fountain, he and Bunion always had cookies for them. When Sarah and Alice said thanks, Bunion would always say, "Momma says, `People got to take care of each other.'"

"Looks like the CO got his new car," said Bubbles waving and laughing.

"Where does he get the money for a car like that?" Bunion breathed.

"My sources say the Park Administrator gave him a good deal. Course we'll probably have to build the Administrator an outhouse or something."

"If I had a car like that, up to home, I could cut up slash wood on some of that old state land. Sell it down to Watertown for stove wood."

"Well, like my momma says, 'If wishes was fishes we'd have some fried.' And you'd ruin the upholstery."

"I could get us through the winter, easy."

"My old man used to get a new Buick every year, until he got shot," said Bubbles.

"Yeah, you told me."

"If we had a car like that, we could sell it for some real cash."

The canteen shared a building with the library and with classrooms. An enrollee presided behind a counter that could be closed off from the rest of the room with a wooden shutter. From there, he sold soft drinks, beer, cigarettes, razor blades and candy bars. A ping pong table, pool table, two card tables and an Esquire calendar made up the rest of the furnishings. Most business was done in cash, but from a cardboard-covered notebook on the counter, the canteen manager also extended credit against enrollees' eight-dollar-a-month allowance.

Two young men were shooting pool. Another sat leaning a chair backward with his feet propped up against the wall as he sipped a beer and watched the game. "What'll it be, Gentleman?" the youth behind the counter greeted the new arrivals.

"Two of your best Simon Pureaquois, barkeep.

"Bubbles, what kind of brew do you want Simon Pure or Iroquois."

"My man, you pick. You're more familiar with the wine cellar here. And put them both on my tab," said Bubbles.

"You're already on the books for six dollars, Bubbles," replied the canteen manager.

"The name is Herby and at ten cents a beer, if my mathematics are correct, that leaves me twenty beers before pay day. Am I right? So rack em up."

"Not for me," said Bunion.

"We got to relax you, you're too tense. Come on, drink up."

The manager had opened two tall brown bottles and set them on the counter. He was busy penciling in the credit book.

"Beer don't set right with me. Sometimes I go crazy," said Bunion.

"Drink your beer. It'll put hair on your chest," said Bubbles. Then under his breath, "Let's see if we can sucker these pool hall turkeys into a real game."

Bubbles succeeded in converting the game on the pool table to craps over the protest of the canteen manager. Then he changed Bunion's dollar at the counter for ten dimes and ran it up to five dollars. As word spread of the game, a small crowd gathered and the stakes drifted upward.

Bunion's heart pounded as he watched the rattling, dancing ivories and so he downed a second beer. He had abstained since a year before when he had gotten ferociously drunk on just two beers. At that time it had appeared to him that the West Carthage softball team had been playing unfairly against his Augustinian Academy nine. After he knocked down three of them, a Sheriff's deputy put him on the ground with a blind side tackle and handcuffed him. Bunion spent that night in the Jefferson County jail.

Now the intoxicating effect of two beers hit him like a runaway freight train. His protests of "Bubbles that's enough," began to slur. "Cash it in, cash it in. Let's go," he insisted through the haze that filled his mind.

But Bubbles seemed transfixed by success. He was playing with other people's money. He was king, boss, emperor as he rattled the dice in his small hand and watched the bets pile up in front of him.

The canteen manager pleaded, "Hey, guys, twenty minutes to lights out. I got to close this joint."

"Keep your shirt on." "There's plenty of time." "We got to get our money back," came from the crowd.

"You're not supposed to play for money in here. It's my butt," he complained.

"Augh, can it." "Quit your belly-aching." "Grow up," Came back at him.

"Shooting the works," Bubbles shouted and pushed out the whole stack. They covered his bet and he rolled a seven.

"Seven, come eleven, cause my baby needs new SHOES," he chanted. "Let her ride, let her rip."

Reluctantly, the crowd covered his bet and Bubbles won again with a seven.

"Bubbles, Bubbles, give me some of that. That's all we need," cried Bunion, choking in the cigarette smoke and reeling with vertigo.

"One more time. One more time, Paul Bunion." Then glancing at his partner, "Gonna' buy you a great blue ox to ride home on PB. Shoot the works, you suckers." Bubbles rattled the dice and flung them tumbling across the green felt of the pool table. They bounded off the cushion rolled and fell still; two black dots surrounded by white stared upward.

"Snake eyes," the crowd roared and grabbed for the money.

Ed Kelly's gleaming blue eyes and red hair popped above the crowd as he jumped to a chair. "Okay, out of here! Captain catches this mess and there'll be extra duty all around---"

"You killjoy, Kelly," an anonymous voice protested.

"And you. Yeah! You. You're going to wind up with brig time," Kelly jammed his finger at the offender.

The canteen manager vaulted the counter and slammed down the shutter, "Closing time, everybody out, now!"

The crowd filed out merrily with their money back in their pockets, except for Bunion and Bubbles. They walked slowly behind. The whistle blew, shrill above the murmur of the retiring men, fifteen minutes to lights-out. Bunion staggered and Bubbles supported him.

"Got to get you to bed, Bunion," said Bubbles guiding him toward the bunkhouse.

"You had---pile of money. Whyn't you quit? Whyn't you give me some?" Bunion mumbled, pulling away.

"Easy come, easy go, old fella. Let's get you to bed."

"There was enough there for, for---"

"Forget it. I got plenty ideas to get money," said Bubbles.

"We had money."

"Couple gals down to Bradford, I know, would love to come up here and earn us some dough."

"You damn rat," said Bunion with unaccustomed violence.

They staggered into the bunk room just in time for Kelly to switch off the lights and the bugler to sound Taps.

"Cripes sakes, for cripes sakes," Bubbles grumbled over and over as he struggled in the dark to get Bunion to lie down fully-dressed on his cot. He threw a blanket over him, then he undressed himself and escaped the gloomy cold under his own blankets.

Bunion, still in his khaki uniform, sat up and stared emptily into the dark. He heard Bubbles' snoring begin. Over and over he pictured that pile of coins and bills on the green felt table top with the dice jumping crazily on it. And he saw his poor skinny old mother in her gray apron at home staring at an empty flour barrel. Then came the vision of Captain Mienecke and his cheerful, healthy family roaring about in their auto-car. Rage swelled inside him, engorging his throat with stifled protest.

Bunion lurched out of bed and crossed the blackened bunk room, miraculously without falling, and silently entered Kelly's office. With one powerful yank, the locked drawer of the wooden desk snapped open. He stuffed Kelly's 45 Colt into his belt and fumbled with the drawer, jamming it back into place at a crooked angle. He moved out across the parade ground in the direction of the barn and Captain Mienecke's prized Reo Flying Cloud Sedan.

A quarter moon that peeked intermittently through Allegany's persistent clouds lit his way into the barn. He wedged his way between the partially-opened barn doors, groped his way to the car, opened the driver's side door and slid behind the wheel, feeling the comfortable luxury of the leather seat beneath him.

He had never, formally, learned to drive but he had seen it done. In his fumbling he found the switch for the headlights. The sudden glare reflected off the gray boards of the barn startled him. He set to trying to start the machine. He tried all the gears and levers he could find but nothing would persuade the engine to turn over. Exasperated, he was about to blow the brains out of the engine with 45 caliber slugs when his eyes fell on a familiar site, a double-bitted felling axe. "Just like up home," he mumbled through gritted teeth.

Bunion took up the great axe with maniacal exaltation. In ten deft blows he had smashed all the windows, hacked a hole in the roof and mashed in the four doors. He took no notice of the laceration to his left forearm, the Reo's revenge, extracted by a shattered window. He left behind a trickle of blood drops as he climbed into the rafters in the far back of the barn's unused hay loft and fell precariously asleep.

Distance and scrub spruce between the barn and the barracks had muffled the noise of Bunion's rampage from most of the men. It woke the nervous Kelly, though. He paused to strap on puttees against rattlers and pull out from under his bunk a four cell flashlight. He stepped into his office for the pistol but could not budge the jammed desk drawer. "Son-of-a-bitch," he said. With the flashlight in one hand, he checked the perimeter of the yard. On his return he announced, to the few who had stirred, "Alright ladies, back to your beds and cover up your heads. Just an old Teddy Bear visiting again. One of these days I'm gonna' have me bear steak for breakfast." To himself he mumbled, "If I can get at my damn gun in time."

Captain Mienecke woke early. He cheerfully strapped on his puttees, found the chamois cloth Mrs. Mienecke had purchased for him and went to the barn to wipe yesterday's grime from his beloved new possession, the Reo Flying Cloud. He strode through the dew of the dim early morning humming "In my merry Oldsmobile---" The big double barn doors gave a good natured screech as he swung them open. Then he saw the wreckage, broken glass and smashed metal. He looked dazed, confused, like a soldier under friendly fire, betrayed. Such unprovoked, wanton destruction was beyond him to understand. The men of the camp liked him and his family. The food was good in camp. The Company was proud of the stone tower they had almost completed and of the road they built. Why begrudge him a second-hand car? A beautiful-second hand car.

A few moments later Kelly was reporting to Mienecke in the Captain's pine-paneled office. Mienecke had been gloomily considering the administrative implication of his wrecked car as he sucked on a pipe and swiveled back and forth behind his government-issue green metal desk. "Enrollee Alton Burroughs is missing, Sir, and I believe he has stolen some property."

"I want to show you something," Captain Mienecke said and he quietly took Kelly into the barn. As they looked at the wrecked car Mienecke asked, "Burroughs, do you think?"

"He is that good with an axe, Sir."

"I can see that, Platoon Leader"

"I just meant---"

"Why would he?"

"I don't know, Sir."

"He's your man."

"He's been worried about money, Sir. I gave him a buck yesterday."

"Against regulations?"

"I know, Sir, but---"

"Where the hell do you suppose he's got to now?"

"Ahem, Sir."

"What?"

"He may---have a Colt 45 automatic with him, Sir."

"A pistol?"

"Mine, Sir---for the snakes."

"Kelly, you idiot, no guns are allowed on Post."

"I know Sir."

"If someone gets shot now---"

Kelly's eye searched the abandoned stalls, the straw-strewn floors and into the dark recesses of the loft. Mienecke followed his gaze and watched as Kelly raised a finger to his lips and pointed at the trail of blood that led toward the loft. Kelly jerked his head toward the door.

Mienecke took his drift instantly. The two men walked quickly out of the barn into safety. Mienecke cleared his throat and stage whispered, "Write this up and have it on my desk in ten minutes, Kelly."

At a safe distance Mienecke turned to Kelly saying, "How are we going to get him out of there without getting someone shot?"

"I don't know, Sir."

"Do you have enough rapport with him to---?"

"Why not burn him out."

"You were too long in the Philippines, Kelly."

Kelly tightened his jaw and said, "Let me get hold of his buddy, that Bubbles guy. Let him go in. Better he gets shot than us."

Mienecke thought, Am I that much of a coward, that I'd order someone else to go in there?   And he thought of his two daughters and his wife. He considered his failure to maintain the order and morale of his command. Then he said, "Okay and if Bubbles has no luck we'll call in the State Police."

All the aggression had drained from Bunion. There was no need for Mienecke's and Kelly's fear of him now. His breath had come short. He was near fainting as Captain Mienecke came in and sighed over the Reo and then came back with Kelly. He exhaled in relief when they had their few words in the barn and left. Concealed in the loft behind a dusty rafter, he huddled like a whipped puppy.   His black hair was mussed, black stubble covered his jaw. His uniform was blood-stained and crumpled. Inside, his head pounded as he recalled, in a blur of remorse, the smashing blows of his axe into the Captain's Reo.

He stared at the pistol lying on the rafter in front of him. What did I want to go and steal that for? That'll send me to jail, sure. What are Ma and Pa going to do then? I'm gonna' have to run for it? Could sell the gun. Ahh, look'a here, I'm bleeding all over the place.

He took out a blue engineer's kerchief and bound the gash in his left forearm. The barn was not far from the cookhouse and the aroma of bacon and coffee began wafting to him. By gollies, I could use a pot of that coffee right now, he thought.

Bubbles sweated in his fresh white apron as he stood in front of a wood-fired cookstove and with a long-handled fork prodded three pounds of thickly-sliced bacon in a tire-sized black iron pan.   The fragrant bacon crackled deliciously in its own meltings. Bubbles eyed Kelly with apprehension as the platoon leader whispered to his protesting boss, the chief cook, and then came toward him, beckoning. "Need your help with a problem, Bubbles. Captain Mienecke wants you in his office, pronto."

"What for? What's this about?"

"Never mind, get that apron off."

"I got breakfast---"

"Get going!" Kelly shouted and the boss cook backed Kelly's order with a wave at Bubbles.

They crossed the parade ground as the bugler sounded reveille. Men poured out of the bunkhouses with towels and soap heading for the wash-house. Bubbles searched the crowd for his charge, Bunion, and he worried.

In Mienecke's office Kelly shoved Bubbles forward, "Sir, this is Enrollee Gortz."

"Yes, I know Bubbles well," Mienecke smiled. "In case my Sarah and Alice forgot, I want to thank you for all those treats."

"My pleasure, Sir," said Bubbles wondering what would follow this pleasantry.

Mienecke went on, "Now, Bubbles, what is it that has gotten into your buddy, Alton Burroughs? They call him Bunion, don't they?

"Eh, yes they do and they call me Herby, Sir."

"Do you have any idea what he's done?"

"No I, no I don't, Sir."

"Have you seen him this morning?"

"He got up ahead of me."

Kelly interrupted, "I ordered you to keep track of him."

"I had to put the coffee and the bacon on." Searching for an explanation he offered, "Sometimes he feeds the raccoons."

"Herby, like the Captain here was trying to tell you, we think he took an axe to the Captain's car."

"Nooo," whined Bubbles.

"An axe," echoed Mienecke.

"While you were supposed to been watching him," Kelly said shaking his head.

"No. He only had two beers. He's not used to it. I put him in his bunk last night to sleep it off. He wouldn't---"

Kelly said, "He did."

"His mom, she didn't get no check, Sir."

"I know---Bubbles, I mean Herby. We think he's hiding up in the barn," Mienecke said.

"There's a trail of blood to the loft," Kelly added.

Bubbles looked quizzically at his superiors, not quite understanding what they wanted of him and suspicious of getting roped in. "Blood? Jees, I'm sorry about him going ape like that. I hope he ain't bad hurt."

"Can you help us out here?" said Mienecke.

"I'd sure like to but I got a ton of bacon that's about to go up in smoke," Bubbles said wringing his greasy hands in his apron. "I got to get back. The guys don't like it burnt."

"Here's the thing, Herby," said Kelly. "He's your friend and we'd like to get him out of the barn---making the least stink out of it that we can. Understand?"

Mienecke said, "Herb, he's got Kelly's Colt 45 automatic. We don't want to see him or anyone else get shot."

"Help us smoke him out of there nice and quiet," said Kelly.

Bubbles did not respond, though his right eyebrow went up automatically as he began to see the situation.

"I would like to keep the State Troopers and the FBI out of this. They could give us all, the whole company, a black eye," Mienecke said shifting uneasily.

Bubbles sensed imminent danger and opportunity. He thought, Old Bunion, he's usually a pretty fair guy. Maybe if I soft soap him just right, he won't shoot me. Make me a hero. Maybe save him some trouble, too.

"So you want me to march in there and tell this guy who just went loony with an axe to come down out of there for breakfast and please don't shoot anyone with that pistol he stole? Is that it?"

"Well, yes. Will you try?"

"Captain, I have been having a little problem getting leave. You see my girl---"

"You will have no problem with leave," said Mienecke.

Five minutes later Bubbles was in the barn carrying a thermos of coffee and surveying the wreckage. He saw the blood drops and followed them slowly toward the loft. "Hey Bunion," he whispered. "You okay? I see some blood here. What a mess you made of this Reo. Hey the medallion on it says it's a "Flying Cloud Sedan. Wow."

He worked his way into the back and up the ladder. "Hey, PB. You in there? It's me, your financial adviser. Where are you?"

"Up here," a cracking voice came from the dark.

"Where?"

"Are you alone?" asked the voice.

"Yeah," answered Bubbles. "Oh, I see you."

"What a mess," said Bunion moving forward on his rafter.

"You or the car?   Look at that uniform. Cripes---You want a coffee?"

"Do I ever, my head is something else."

The two enrollees emerged from the barn into a bright fresh morning.   The sun had risen above the cookhouse and dew twinkled on the grass of the parade ground.   Captain Mienecke, Doctor Phelps, Kelly and another Platoon Leader greeted the pair warily and led them into Mienecke's office.   Bunion's head was down and way to the right side.   Bubbles carried the 45 by its barrel.   He handed it gingerly to Kelly who, in a smart military fashion, ejected and reinserted the full clip of shells, clicked the safety to the on position and placed the pistol in a grenade bag over his shoulder.

That afternoon Bunion and Bubbles were sitting on a bench outside the cook house peeling and quartering potatoes from a gunny sack and tossing them into a galvanized steel garbage can half full of water.   "That was real smart of you to say you were going to pay for the damage to Mienecke's car," said Bubbles. "Where are you going to get that kind of cash?"

"I meant, I wished I could pay for it.   I ain't got a cent. Looks like I never will have."

"You could be a prize fighter.   You cold-cocked that stone cutting bastard.   He must a went two-fifty."

"He shouldn't of got me mad.   I ain't accountable when I'm mad."

"Like when you're drinking, that's the 'patho-something' Doc said you had."

"Panther-logical Intoxication.   Means I got a bad temper and I go crazy if I get a whiff of booze."

"So we give you a little swig before a fight.   It would be no worse than dopin' a horse."

"Look what those two beers got me into. No thank you."

"You do what you did to the Reo, to Joe Louis and everything'll be hunky-dory. Why don't you let me help you make some money, instead of trouble, with those mitts? I made a good thing out of managing Golden Gloves when I was in the home and I---"

"No booze for me, period."

"Just an idea. On the booze, I was too busy looking after our finances to nursemaid you."

"Busy losing my money." Bunion stood up and pitched the potato he had been peeling into the galvanized can creating a splash that Bubbles had to dodge.

"Watch it, wise guy," Bubbles yelled.

"You know I hate this KP detail. How do you stand this every single day?"

"No snakes, all you want to eat, steak any time of the day, no sunburn."

"Stuck in camp all day long, never seeing nothing but people and buildings, no fresh air."

"See that you don't go running off for no fresh air, now. The only reason you're not in the Salamanca hoosegow, breathing mildew, is because I said I'd keep an eye on you. Now you sit tight and peel those spuds."

Bunion stared across the parade ground in the direction of the stone fountain, where Sarah and Alice, the Mienecke kids, were giggling and splashing each other. "You said no snakes in camp?" he exclaimed.

"What'd you say?" Bubbles did not understand Bunion's sudden change in tone of voice and posture.

Bunion grabbed for the eighteen-inch butcher knife they had been using to quarter potatoes. "Rattler," he said pointing at the girls with the knife but not moving.

Bubbles saw the timber rattler, coiled, ready to defend itself against Sarah's backward tread. She laughed and retreated slowly. Bubbles whispered, "I'll go for Kelly's gun."

"No time."

"You got the knife, kill it," Bubbles urged.

Bunion, knife in hand, loped quietly toward the girls.

Bubbles, with a half-peeled potato in one hand, scooped up the sack with the other as he moved cautiously forward.

Kelly and Mienecke were stepping off the porch of Mienecke's office. They saw Bunion, with the knife, running in the direction of the girls.

"God damn that man," yelled the Captain leaping toward his daughters.

Kelly methodically extracted the 45 from the grenade sack around his shoulder, knelt, took the grip in both hands and tracked two feet in front of Bunion.

Bunion heard Mienecke swear, saw Kelly level the Colt at him and realized the berserk image they saw. "They got me nuts," he thought. He crouched and dodged still intent on the safety of the girls.

Bubbles yelled as he saw Kelly sink into his firing stance, "Don't shoot, don't shoot." Diving and rolling out of the firing line he threw the potato at Kelly.

Kelly had flicked the safety on his weapon and begun a firm slow pressure on its trigger. The potato arched through the air. Bubbles was up on his knees shouting, "Kelly! Snake!" and the wet raw potato slammed into Kelly's ear. The gun went off, throwing its slug into the kitchen, alarming the KP crew but hurting no one. Bunion flinched at the report of the gun, but swept the blade of the knife toward the snake and severed its head. He tripped, sprawled alongside the snake's writhing body and snapped away from it with revulsion. Leaping to his feet, he stamped and kicked at it.

Running, Mienecke, finally grasping the situation, yelled at Kelly, "No, no," and waved him off with both arms. He raced to the girls and scooped them up.

Kelly lowered the gun, replaced it in the grenade bag and approached the excited group at the fountain.

"My God, Bunion, I didn't know what you were doing," Mienecke shouted.

"Daddy, don't swear," ordered Sarah.

Bunion gazed into Kelly's still unblinking eyes, shook his head and spat, then turned to Mienecke and said, "Bad lookin' snake. When Pa had a team, rattler, 'bout that size, bit the off gray. We didn't get no use out of them for a month."

"Where's his head, Daddy? Can we touch him, Daddy? Can we play with him?" said the girls one after the other.

"Better let the snake alone," said Mienecke. Then he said to Bunion, "Thanks, thanks, that was wonderful. I didn't know what you were doing. You were running with that knife."

"Sometimes you can tail-grab them and snap their head into a rock. I didn't want to give him that chance, Sir."

"Thank you, thank you so much and we'll take this into consideration when we figure out what to do about those charges."

"If you could just get the pay clerk to send that check up home, Sir."

"I'll see it is tended to, personally. And maybe we can forget that whole other thing. We are even and then some."

"No ,Sir, I plan to pay for those damages."

"We'll see, we'll see," said Mienecke.

Alice, looking as if she was tiring of the excitement already said, "Bubbles, got anything to eat? Bubbles, I'm hungry." Bubbles reached into the pocket of his now-soiled apron and found two banged-up molasses cookies for the girls.

Alice gobbled hers but Sarah took her cookie, and quietly handed it to Bunion, "Like you said about your Momma, people got to take care of each other. This one is for you."

"They sure do, Ma'm." Bunion stuffed the cookie, whole, into his jaw, straightened his head and grinned.

Epilogue:

All four of these men served in the Army's 1st Infantry Division, known as the Big Red One. On 8 November 1942 they entered World War II on the North African coast of Algeria in the first American campaign against Germany.

Bunion served a month in the Salamanca Jail. For a time the Park administration made a considerable effort to ban the sale of beer. He trained as a boxer in the Army and after WWII had some success as a light heavyweight in the professional ring before returning to work the family farm.

Bubbles drove a CCC truckload of "surplus" flour, bacon and potatoes up to Carthage that fed Bunion Burroughs' family through that month and that winter. He married a girl from Bradford and with her family opened Bradford's first drive-in theater.

Kelly became a supply officer. After WWII he established the largest Army surplus store in Manhattan.

The Mieneckes visited the Burroughs' family on their farm for a week each summer for many years.

Don't Throw $1,500,000 Down Abandoned Oil Wells 1997

Commissioner Bernadette Castro's Office of Parks, Recreation and Historic Preservation (OPRHP) wants to plug 70 abandoned oil wells in Allegany State Park at a cost of $20,000 a well. The system she proposes, re-drilling each well and plugging it with concrete, is wasteful overkill. The threat of these wells to the environment and to people is minimal. In fact, chances are very good that the operators of these wells plugged them fifty years ago.

Commissioner Castro, all that we need to ensure the safety of those wells, at a fraction of the cost you propose, are a few good men with shovels or one with a backhoe. Remember that it has taken Allegany a hundred years to recover from the last oil well-drilling stampede.

In 1894, Job Moses drilled a hole into a mountainside in what is now Allegany State Park. His gusher, the first commercial oil well in New York State, produced sixty barrels a day and kicked off a boom. Pennzoil followed him and turned the woods into an oil field.

On the old Limestone Road into the Park, there is a stone monument erected to commemorate Job. He doesn't need that monument. He left us 200 abandoned oil and gas wells to remind us of his good fortune.

Over the last 20 years, Commissioner Castro's Department has quietly plugged 130 of those abandoned wells. On April 29 of this year, I attended an informational meeting that she arranged at Camp Allegany. There OPRHP Officials described her proposal to spend 1.5 to 2 million unnecessary dollars to plug the remaining 70 wells.

Each well would need the woods cut down for a clearing wide enough to erect a drilling rig and to park a cement mixer and a dump truck. To get this gear to the wells, Commissioner Castro would have to cut five-and-a-half miles of 20 to 30 foot-wide-road through the woods.

Abandoned oil well

A week later two of us walked these wells with Terry Dailey, the Park Forester. They are off the beaten track, among the remote pitches and gullies of Allegany's Rice Brook and Mount Irvine. These are places where only an occasional hunter might pass. Even with pink ribbons cueing our way to the wells, Terry had to search to show them to us.

We started off, in view of the house-sized, moss-covered gray masses of Thunder Rock, down an old road now used as a horse and snowmobile trail. Shortly, we were bushwhacking where Commissioner Castro intends to cut roads.

Purple Spring Beauties carpeted the floor of the woods and in wet places succulent skunk cabbage grew. The trees are substantial second-growth hardwoods, eighty to ninety years old.

Only suggestions of the old oil well roads were visible in the regenerating forest. It was easy to imagine bulldozers ripping them open again.

Deep in the woods, two porcupines squatted with their backs toward us threatening with their spiky, white-tipped quills.

When we approached, they waddled off to scamper up trees, their mobile black faces and hands making them look like monkeys. They are one of the few creatures an unarmed man can kill in the woods. Woodsmen cherish them and kill them only when starving.

I doubt that this pair would survive the truck traffic Commissioner Castro proposes for their sanctuary.

The Park has marked almost all the wells and fenced several that are near trails. The standard holes we found were woodchuck-sized at the top. We saw only one that was large enough to fall into.

We came away from the hike skeptical of Commissioner Castro's proposal. A week later we confirmed our doubts with a crash course in "applied petroleum engineering" from Department of Environmental Conservation (DEC) oil specialists. Here are Commissioner Castro's reasons for plugging the abandoned wells in Allegany State Park:

1. Danger to animals and people as pitfalls.

2. Contamination of the surface with oil and of aquifers with surface water or with oil.

3. A financial window of opportunity made by the Environmental Bond Act and other sources.

4. A boost to the Cattaraugus County economy. Private contractors would do the work over the next several years, providing nine jobs.

5. There is a law that requires owners to plug abandoned wells.

Commissioner Castro's representatives also gave this disturbing opinion. "Obviously, plugging the wells would improve the environment, therefore no formal EIS (Environmental Impact Study) would be necessary." They referred to an important provision of SEQR (The State Environmental Quality Review Law).

To make these arguments and come to this conclusion, I must conclude that whoever is doing the deciding at OPRHP has never walked those woods or talked with the DEC oil experts who have.

When I talked to those experts this is what I heard:

1. The DEC, the enforcer of the well-plugging law in New York State, is not requiring the Park to plug those wells.

2. Of the tens of thousands of old abandoned wells in New York State, DEC requires plugging only when there is evidence of oil spillage at the surface or evidence of subsurface water contamination.

3. There is no such evidence of oil leakage or water contamination by the Park wells, even after 50 years of abandonment.

4. In any case, once a water well has been contaminated with oil, plugging the guilty oil well does not correct the condition.

5. The danger of people falling into these wells is very unlikely and could be completely eliminated by a simple sand and rock filling of the hole. (Personal inspection of the wells tells us that anything bigger than a woodchuck would have trouble crawling into all but a very few of them.)

6. The New York State Flooding Law of 1919, which was in effect when these wells went out of operation, required their plugging, "for the purpose of excluding [all] water from gas-bearing rock." DEC officers told us that the system of plugging required then was an effective and lasting one.

7. The Park wells were owned by the large, reputable, Pennzoil Corporation. If OPRHP believes that those wells are not plugged then they must assume that Pennzoil broke the law.

These wells have been in place a hundred years and no one has fallen into one of them. The Park is marking them and fencing the larger ones. OPRHP tells us that the wells are up to 1400 feet deep. But they fail to explain that about 1380 feet of that depth is an eight-inch-wide hole in bedrock into which no person can fall. The eight-inch hole, above bedrock, goes through 20 to 30 feet of soil that may erode into something larger. We saw only one into which a person could fall.

Let's not take a chance. Let's plug the few obvious holes with rock and sand. Last month I sat in on a Civilian Conservation Corps reunion in the Park. When those guys were in their prime, three of them with shovels could have sealed a well in a day.

There are better ways to spend Environmental Bond Act money: outside the Park, we have toxic waste sites to be cleaned and landfills to be closed, inside new cabins on Dowd Trail would be a blessing.

Allegany's oil-boom scar has almost healed. Let's not turn Rice Creek and Mount Irvine back into the industrial wasteland that Job Moses kicked off a hundred years ago.

Allegany January

It's Friday afternoon January 11. I'm driving up the snowy incline from Salamanca into Allegany State Park. There at the summit of South Mountain the superb Art Roscoe Ski area beckons me. The time is 3:30. Sunset is at 4:30. I want to get some skiing in before dark.

Art Roscoe in the Toque

The sky is overcast and snow forms a scrim over the view of Salamanca below. The woods are bare of leaves but snow on the forest floor makes trees stand out like the charcoal strokes of an artist. I murmur, "Goodbye, city life."

I may be the first of the ADK (Adirondack Mountain Club) skiers to arrive this weekend but I'll check in at Red House Administration Building later. Gotta' get some skiing in while there's light.

Quick into my boots. Don't forget the GPS unit (Global Positioning System) and the brand new cell-phone. Got some high-tech stuff to mess with this weekend.

At the entrance to the ski area the Park has a six by four-foot, engraved wooden trail map. I study it. Sweetwater Loop looks good. It's the only one marked with a circle meaning "easy." My creaky right hip says, better stay away from the ones marked with the black diamonds, till we see how things go.

Sweetwater is three miles long. Good, I can do that in an hour and beat sundown. But first there is the GPS thing. I pull off the two layers of mittens on my right hand and take the GPS in my palm. This thing eats batteries, so I have supplied it with a fresh pair. It has fooled me by mixing old data with new so I have deleted everything and left it turned off till now when I, not just it, am ready to navigate. The GPS is on and blinking at me as it claims it is trying to lock in four orbiting satellites. "Are you indoors?" it asks. I push the "no" button, hard. OK, it's got "lock." I push another couple buttons to "mark a waypoint" (that's GPS talk) here at the trail sign. If all goes well it will lead me back here.

The air is cool. The new snow sticks to my skis at first. That's great for walking uphill but slows me on the flat and downhill.

There's a snowmobile track. Some guy must have got lost looking for the back door of the Red Garter. At night, lit up like a Las Vegas Casino, that restaurant looms over the road I just ascended.

Might as well plug another waypoint into the GPS. Yikes, it claims my speed hit 35 miles an hour. I must have been hanging on to that snowmobile?

I push off down the snowy trail. Allegany's 80 to 90-year-old beeches, maples and ash are getting a leg on toward an impressive forest. I glide smoothly and quickly through these darkening woods. The sticking is gone.

Here and there I see a bed of leaves and disturbed snow where a deer has slept and lots of hoof prints. These stealthy denizens aren't showing themselves tonight. Plenty of squirrel and chipmunk tracks, too. A hawk soars above looking for an unwary dinner.

In the car I glance at the GPS. The map it has drawn of my route looks nothing like the loop I know I skied. It's a straight line, ridiculous.

I load my sleeping bag and extra clothes into one of the two bunkrooms in number 8, the men's cabin for tonight. It's a hotel compared to the uninsulated one-room shanties I remember loving as a kid. We've got electric-powered heat, stove and refrigerator.

I was hoping Art and Jay would show up to go to dinner with me. They don't, so I head for town on my own. Meyers is jammed. But the restaurant does itself proud. A charming waitress serves me a bowl of salad-vegetables and a basket of hot rolls. "That'll keep you busy," she says. She takes my order and quickly brings Manhattan clam chowder with chunks of chewy clams. She apologizes. Because of the crowd there will be a wait for the rest. I wallow in the flavor of fish and tomatoes. I make a couple trips to the bar for bowls of popcorn. There I discover "hors d'oeuvres," submarine sandwiches cut into fist-sized chunks. I help myself. Then my broccoli, baked potato and sizzling slab of broiled haddock arrive. I pass on the apple pie. The bill comes to eleven dollars.

By the time I get back to the cabin, Jay, John and Art have moved in. Art says, "Hey Buddy, you missed a great fish fry. We stopped at the Ellicottville Hotel." He is a burly, bearded, good-natured ex-farm kid who has wound up his career working for the Army Corps of Engineers. "A little pricey though," he adds.

"Yeah, it was good but I haven't had many $20 fish fries," says Jay.

So I have a great time telling them what they missed down at Meyers, "The submarines and the popcorn, alone, were worth the $10 I paid for the dinner."

John gives us bad news, "JoAnn canceled the wine and cheese party."

On my way to the outhouse, the electrically-heated, brilliantly-lit, cinderblock outhouse with the flush-toilets and hot showers (I've heard of some people being described as "built like a brick privy." Well, this is either a Mae West or Arnold Schwarzenegger of an outhouse.) I meet JoAnn, the trip organizer. She is headed in the opposite direction. "Hi, Larry. You all moved in and comfortable?" she yawns. She, her husband David and the other girls are in our second cabin. David and JoAnn met on one of these trips. Jay introduced them.

"We're all set," I say. "But no wine and cheese party?"

"No, David and I go to bed early. We like to sit around in our jammies." She pauses, "But you can come over if you want. Please come over. We have a bottle of wine and some excellent brie."

"I'll pass it by the rest of the crew."

A few minutes later, in the men's cabin, we are sitting around the table shooting the breeze about food. Art has just measured out a half peck of oatmeal that he is going to boil for breakfast. "I buy it by the 50 pound sack and sell it like this for a dollar a bag." He holds up a plastic bagful the size of a Quaker oats carton.

John says, "I always take oatmeal on a canoe trip, but did you ever try that Red River cereal? It has those flaxseeds in it. I like it for variety."

Then they were off on camp cookery. I had to put my own twist on it. "You know, the best camp food I've ever had was fresh caught fish."

Art recalls, "My uncle took me fishing up to Muskoka once. We stopped at the commissary. All he bought for us for lunch was bread and butter. But when we caught those trout, he skinned them, built a fire, laid them out on pieces of slate, and we ate them in sandwiches with the bread and butter. They were so good."

Just then JoAnn poked her head in the door. "Hi. How you all doing? You coming over? We've got the bottle open and a whole bunch of stuff from Premier (the gourmet food store). Anybody like garlic olives?" We all bundled off across the snow to cabin 9.

I delay a moment on the way. Time to make my first ever call on a cell-phone. Now, with this thing, if the GPS doesn't work, I can call in air support.

I'm set for speed dialing. Just push the number 2 for home. Hope Lyn picks up.

" Huh!" What's this on the screen? "Call cannot be completed."

Inside by the wine bottle are oriental-seasoned humus, an assortment of English crackers, rye-crisps and the cheddar and brie. After I settle in and nibble a couple of those garlic-stuffed olives, Art tells me, "Last year I had to go way up on the hill to get my cell-phone connected. I had to hold the thing up in the air." He looks at mine and says "Didn't you pull the antenna out?" He tugs dangerously at the non-extendable antenna on my obviously sub-par device before I put it out of reach and change the subject.

Us old codgers make plans for a couple easy hours skiing in the morning, rest up after lunch and do an hour or so in the late afternoon.

The young tigers are huddled over maps, jabbing fingers. "Let's take that cut-off along the ridge over to Thunder Rock," David says.

The conversation continues fairly lively till someone notices that our hosts have turned in. Then we are off to bed. It is a brisk dark night. Snow is still falling. The lights of our Summit Cabin windows throw Christmas-card shafts of illumination across the snow.

Next morning Art is up early, stirring a mighty pot of oatmeal. He has honey, raisins and gallons of milk to go with it. Ehmm, smell that coffee brewing. I have my own packets of instant cereal but Art insists we join him. John is up soon, then Jay. Late arrival, Paul, comes knocking at the door in time to help out, too. We are all responsible for our own meals except for the one smorgasbord Saturday night but Art, like a mother hen, is taking care of us all.

Paul picks up the honey jar. He is big, has a round face and wears a moustache. He lives on a farm, talks like it, but has spent most of his life behind a desk working for the New York State Employment Service. He reads us the honey label, "Pure Black Buckwheat Honey." He extemporizes, "I used to have seven hives. Planted a patch of buckwheat near them. Figured I'd have buckwheat honey to sell. I couldn't give the stuff away. It was black, like this. Everyone thought there was something wrong with it." He then held forth very informatively, on the art of honey culture, with little urging from us.

"Did ya ever get stung?" I ask.

"Yes, but after a few stings, they don't swell anymore. It's just like getting a needle stuck in you. Of course you wear a net. There is always one sucker that gets up inside and takes his time while he finds the tenderest part to stick you."

Listening, I get up from the table to put a coat of glide-wax on my skis. Art and Paul are still drinking coffee and talking about anything they can think of to keep from skiing. So I go off on my own heading for the view off the Christian Hollow loop.

This warming hut at Summit was once the fire tower cabin

By noon I'm back at the empty cabin to eat my peanut butter-and-jelly, bagel sandwich. Guess the rest of them did finally go skiing after all. The air inside is redolent of onions, cabbage, tomatoes, beef and something sour. I taste Paul's chili, simmering on the stove. Very little pepper. Excellent. Art has something curious brewing in a crock-pot. I take a peak. Let it cook a while.

The only convenient system for toasting my bagels seems to be putting them directly on one of the burners of the electric stove. I'm a little guilty about it but who's to know? In just a moment I hear fumbling and mumbling at the door and then pounding. I'm busy watching the toast and I yell, "What's up? Come on in."

Paul yells back, "You've got the door locked."

"No it's not. Try again."

He's grumbling and thumping out there. I start for the door. All of a sudden there is the hideous shriek of a beeping. Holy cow, has Paul called the Park Police? I lunge to the door. It's not locked. It opens easy as pie. There are Paul and Art. Art's laughing, "What kind of a cook are you? You burned the toast. You set off the smoke alarm."

When I'm almost done eating my charcoal sandwich, Art is still chewing on his slab of corned beef between two chunks of New York rye. He is eyeing a schedule of Park events while also debating the NAFTA protests with Paul. It's gonna' be a while before I can change the subject to, what's in the crock-pot? I peer over Art's shoulder. "Dog sled racing at 12 noon," I read on the schedule.

Paul is saying, "750,000 jobs, gone south of the border."

Art says, "EPA regulations won't tolerate the furniture industry's running a paint line like that up here so they take off to Mexico and pollute all they want."

I leave them gnawing on that and head for the dogs. What a beautiful day this has turned into, bright sun, blue sky, wisps of clouds and great snow on the ground.

A small crowd waits across from the horse trailer area on ASP 2 (Allegany State Park Highway 2). Spare sled dogs are tied to the bumpers of pickups. These dogs are smaller than I expect, about 40 pounds. They are a nondescript lot, not typical Nanuk-of-the-North type huskies. One mutt peers at me with just his head showing above the flat bed of a trailer, his eyes, the palest blue, his pointed black ears lined in white stand at the alert as he waits for one false move from me.

Sled dog

An official with a two-way radio and a bullhorn dangling from his neck is spray- painting a finish line in the snow, signal orange. He claims to the crowd, "The dogs like it". As if in response, the dogs that were left behind start whimpering and barking. Something comes in on the radio. The official lifts his head. "Here they come."

The first team crosses the bridge, rounds the turn and heads down the straightaway dead at us. They are silent, red tongues hanging from their furry mouths. They bound in their traces, tugging with a will but they are running low on steam. The driver urges them on, one foot on a runner, the other pumping the snow.

Here come Art and Paul. Looks like the post-NAFTA conference is over.

We watch the other teams finish. I follow the team of greyhounds to their station wagon. Their driver is thin and rangy like the dogs. He's smiling, exhilarated and a little short of wind. "They sure all look related," I say.

He says proudly. "All seven from the same litter. The eighth is home with a broken hip. I've got their ma and grandma too, three generations."

"Are they greyhounds?"

"Yes, but mixed with Labrador and setter."

I see now that they have longer hair than typical greyhounds and slightly heavier lines. Someone told me he carries all his dogs in that little gray station wagon he is tying them to. I hope for a picture but I am distracted.

The popcorn man has arrived. He stands by a cauldron, wooden paddle in hand, stirring. He opens the throttle on the gas burner and a powerful "oomph" accompanies a burst of blue flame from under it and a delicious odor drifts by. A batch of kettle corn is ready. Art and Paul arrive at his side first. I mosey over, hoping for a sample of this delicious salty-sweet concoction

"Try some, you'll love it," says the Popcorn Man, offering a dishful of his wares.

I accept, sweeping a generous supply into two hands with, "Thanks." Yes, I know." I munch it down.

Art tries a handful, too, and grins. "Give me one of those he says" pointing at the four dollar, not the two dollar "teaser" bag.

I was set to be satisfied with the free sample but I have to save Art from himself. "I'll buy half," I offer.

He nods half-heartedly, and pockets my two dollars. We pass the bag back and forth; feed some to Paul and to Grace

Christy, the Park naturalist, who appears out of nowhere. "Ehmm it's good," I say.

"Wait till you taste my Salyanka tonight." Art says.

"What's that?" says Paul.

"Why this guy here," he points to me, "claimed I was trying to poison him with too much chili pepper in my chili so I'm making Armenian Salyanka for tonight."

"But what is it?" Paul says.

"Smelled awful interesting up there in camp," I say.

"My Irish grandmother's version is leftover corned beef and cabbage, scallions and potatoes all mashed up and boiled together, then made into patties and fried. But it's probably too greasy for you guys. Tonight is going to be Mid-Eastern style. I've cut up potatoes, onions and cabbage and they are stewing together. Well, I didn't have yogurt so I put in cottage cheese and vinegar and a few spices, some rosemary and stuff. You'll love it. It's gonna' be good."

I'm thinking, Paul's got this big pot of chili and Art's putting so much effort into whatever that is he's making, maybe the loaf of banana bread, Lyn made for my contribution is not enough. She makes a mean banana bread. I could eat the whole thing myself. I had better go into town and buy a few submarine sandwiches.

In Salamanca I find the supermarket. Yes, they have subs but they also have whole barbequed chickens. I buy a chicken. What an elegant impression it will make for me at dinner. Salyanka? Ha!

I have time for a ski. Christian Hollow was good; I'll run it the other way. The snow is setting up. It's fast. I feel it in the hip a touch. Back at the cabin the cooking smells are more impressive than ever. I make a trip to our most outstanding of outhouses for a shower. It's warm but not as hot as I crave. On the way back JoAnn sticks her head out of her cabin door. "Six PM for dinner, right?" she calls.

"I'm ready," I answer.

Six PM and eight of us are crowded into our cabin's main room. Dave lugged over an extra bench. Our counters, table and stove are laden with bread, cheese, chicken, a heaping pile of salad, chips and dips, chili, macaroni, candy, cake, pie, banana bread, roast chicken, two bottles of wine and a crock pot of Salyanka. We could winter over.

At first the conversation is subdued as each one ladles food onto his plate and begins feeding. I surreptitiously taste Paul's chili again. Yes, I think it is mild enough for me. So I take a helping and dilute it with two parts of macaroni and cheese.

My chicken sits there with no one showing interest. I'm terrible at carving. No one volunteers to work on it so I take out my Swiss army knife and do some major surgery. There is considerable interest in the white meat.

I have a spare bowl so I venture a look at Art's pride. It is pale white and has a strong hard-to-pin-down odor. Manfully I place several spoonfuls in my dish. The Salyanka is not to my taste, though I try it more that once. I hear little comment about this new dish, even from Art, though the other dishes are roundly applauded. He has some of it on his plate. He toys with it, sniffs at a spoonful and as he places it in his mouth his lip curls to the right. He gulps and moves on to the chili. My heart goes out to him while I quietly inter my portion of Salyanka in an empty cocoa can.

Lyn's banana bread goes over big.

Now, it's Sunday afternoon. I'm in my car back at the Salamanca overlook. Let's make one more stab at the cell-phone; call home. A long distance operator comes on and wants to charge me for "roaming."

I have had enough of roaming. I'm heading home for Lyn's Sunday dinner.

Snowmobile Trail in Art Roscoe X-C Ski Area 1998
No Environmental Impact Study

I stopped to take in that view of Salamanca tucked into its green valley. I was enjoying the woods as I drove up the mountain into Allegany State Park. Then just a mile before the entrance to the Summit cross-country ski area, I caught my breath in disbelief. Someone had piled fifty red pine logs, each 10 to 12 inches in diameter, at the side of the road. I got out and walked into the woods aghast at the stumps and destruction.

Governor Pataki promised us over a year ago that there would be no logging in Allegany State Park and he promised us a Park Master Plan to guarantee that. The plan remains buried, most say until after the elections. Yet the New York State Environmental Review Act (SEQR) and the National Environmental Protection Act are in effect.

How could it happen that the Park Administration built a road (they call it a trail but it is as wide as the blacktop highway it intersects) through our woods without any announcement, without public debate, without an environmental impact statement under the SEQR law and in disregard for the value of an intact, maturing forest?

Abominable Snowmobile Trail

Sierra and the Adirondack Mountain Club have called them to account. The Park explained lamely that it just slipped by; they were busy at the time. They have, however, halted the construction but only after cutting down a few thousand trees in a mile-long 30-foot wide sweep. The uncompleted portion of this "thruway" through the woods remains surveyed and tagged in signal orange over some steep and wooded terrain to its objective, the back door of the Red Garter Tavern on the edge of Salamanca.

Allegany State Park is 60,000 acres of forest that has been undisturbed for 90 to 350 years. It's a park. In a way it is a museum. It towers alone, as such, in the midst of hundreds of thousands of acres of forests in Western New York and in Pennsylvania that are managed for timber harvesting. The potential giants of those other forests are never allowed to live out their lives, mature and die in place, to return their nutrients to the soil from which they were borrowed.

Allegany is a glorious woods where old hemlocks grow four feet across and vault to cathedral heights. White, pine, maple, black cherry and beech are there reaching full size. Really ancient trees die in the Park sprouting huge white dinner plate fungus. Squirrels, raccoons and Pileated woodpeckers make homes in the blackness of their hollowed trunks. Giant trees fall in the silent wood and molder under carpets of green moss while tiny spotted orange salamanders scamper over them. This full length forest process holds water in place, keeps streams clear and aquifers full, while turning carbon dioxide back into oxygen for us to breath. It is a beautiful, exemplary place, a well-beloved refuge from man's abuse of the world that nurtures and cherishes us.

Allegany has 90 miles of snowmobile trails

I call for a full SEQR assessment of the environmental impact of this half-completed new Park "trail". I call for public hearings on the issue and for the scientific opinion of forest ecologists.

That cut through the woods should be abandoned as a trail and replanted in trees.

Big Surprise Down in the Woods

Brad Whitcomb, our new Allegany State Park Forester, stands in the wood-paneled great-room of the Red House Administration Building. The mounted head of a local ten-point buck adorns the wall behind him and the antlers of a Wyoming elk form a seven-foot arc over the stone fireplace. Windows offer a panorama of lake and forest-covered mountains. But the crowd's eyes are on Brad. We are eager to hear from this man with the reputation for black bears. Everyone has a bear story in mind. We are in the mood for a Teddy Bear's Picnic:

> If you go down in the woods to day,
> You're in for a big surprise.
> Today's the day
> The Teddy bears have their picnic.

Brad is a big, tall guy with a gray speckled beard and shoulders and profile that would serve well in Hollywood. He has an easy laugh and friendly, approachable style. He's the daddy bear today and his ranger-job is to, without spoiling the romance, break some news about bears. The big surprise down in the woods is that black bears are not Teddy bears. They are great big, powerful eating and sex machines.

Here's my version of how Brad put this across.

"I'm the new forester," he said. "I've worked here in the Park twenty-five years, started in maintenance, went to college in Wisconsin, and got a degree in Biology and Environmental Science. In seventy-two, while I was in school, I got to work with a fella' named Lynn Rogers, the Minnesota black bear expert. Anytime you see anything about black bears on TV it's usually Lynn. By that time, he had already collared and monitored 70 bears. He had to capture and tranquilize them, measure them and pull a tooth. We were there to help.

"There'd be four foot of snow on the ground. We'd be on snowshoes. A warm day would be ten degrees. You'd come on a den and hear the cubs, sounded like a litter of puppies. We had to go into each den and change the batteries on the bear's collar.

Kodiak Grizzly and Cub

"My first time out with him, Lynn said, 'Ok, you go first.'

"'What?' I said.

"'Go in and count the cubs.

"'Don't we… put 'em to sleep first?

"'No, no, she's asleep.

Brad leaned over holding an imaginary flashlight at an angle behind his head. "A bear cave is not a big hole. I had my flashlight. I think it needed new batteries. Lynn said, 'Any movement from her, you wiggle your feet. We'll pull you out.

"I got in there. All I could see was this big bear head, eyes wide open looking at me. I wiggled my feet.

Brad lowered the flashlight abruptly and stood upright.

"'How many pups?' he asked me.

"'She's awake!

"Lynn went in, gave her a shot of PCP, angel dust. It's not legal anymore. Makes you hallucinate. I think of all the trips we must have sent those bears on.

He shook his head.

"Lynn sent me back in and I brought out the two cubs. They looked like little moles with their eyes shut tight. The female weighed one pound, the male a pound and four ounces. Then we had to pull their mom out and measure her. When we were done, we put the cubs back in first, so they wouldn't wander off before she woke up. Had to kind of stuff her in as far as we could. She only weighed two fifty or so. You get a seven-hundred-pound male and you need a tractor to pull him out and you don't get him back in.

"Lynn usually went into the male bear caves, himself. He never took any protection, claimed he'd never been hurt. There was a bar up there in Minnesota we used to go to. We told the bartender that and he gave us a look, said 'Well, Lynn's come in here more than one time, bloodied up.

Bob Schmid, squinting through his camera sight as he eagerly videotapes from the audience, asks Brad, "Did Charlie John ever tell you about the guy who got hurt trying to push a bear into his car? He wanted a picture of him behind the steering wheel.

"Yes, I heard about that. We haven't had any bear bites lately but every year we get patrons bitten by raccoons. Last year a guy tried to shoo a porcupine out of his car. The porky was chewing on the steering wheel. The guy knocked the clutch out of gear and the car rolled down the hill into a ditch. We had to take him to the hospital.

"Lynn tried to give us a healthy respect for bears. One of his favorite stories was about a friend of his. This friend found a bear wandering around, kind of dazed, in his backyard with his head stuck inside of a milk can. He roped him, by one foot, to a tree. That ticked the bear. The guy ran up to pull the can off. The bear lunged, broke the rope. He was only a two-hundred-pound bear but a two-hundred-pound bear is terribly strong. Darn near killed him. Lynn had some horrible pictures of the guy's wounds."

In the pause after this story I start wondering if Brad did any climbing down into bear dens around here. I ask him, "Have you collared any bears in the Park?"

He answered, "Three to four years ago the DEC collared and released two bears down here. One of them slipped his off and we found it. The other one was shot over in Quaker next season. The reason for going to the trouble of putting a radio collar on a bear is to learn where they live, what they are eating and how far they'll travel to find mates. Then we can make plans about how to get along with them. We didn't learn much off those two."

Bob Sieben raises his hand respectfully and asks, "How many bears would you guess there are in the Park?"

"I don't know," Brad answers and pauses. "I could guess 20 or 40, and be high or low. I worked for years here in the Park, and never saw a bear. The population is up. I understand just last week there was a problem bear up around Buffalo. He probably wandered in from Pennsylvania. It's spring time and young male fancy turns to 'just that one thing.' He's looking for it. The DEC trapped him and took him back toward the PA line. They pointed him in the right direction and shot him in the butt with a rubber bullet.

"In the five counties that make up the Allegany Bear District, in the 2001 season hunters took 60 bears. That's five more than the previous year and twice the ten year average. There're more bears around, but last year we also had an open winter and late hibernation. There was a good crop of nuts so the bears stayed up late eating.

"Black bear is what they call them, but they're not all black. Some are brown. Males are aggressive, especially during mating season and they have a wide range. They are born at about a pound and, full-grown, can weigh seven or eight-hundred pounds. Average life expectancy is twenty years.

"Sows only carry as many cubs to term as they have the nutrition to support. They have an unusual floating embryo system. A sow may have four fertilized eggs but somehow her body will judge how much she has eaten and abort the embryos she can't handle. They only have a litter every other year. When you pull a tooth you can count the rings of calcium deposit, one heavy and one light, to calculate how many litters she's had.

"A bear is one of the few animals that will adopt a strange cub. Last year I got a call from the Park Police over in Quaker Run. 'Come on over here, we got four bears up in trees and everybody's out takin' pictures. We got a traffic jam.

"It was a female and three cubs. Those weren't all her own; she must have adopted at least one of them. She and the cubs had been wandering over there by the garbage and somebody's dog scared her. She went up a tree and the cubs followed her. She'd never come down with all that crowd and it was too hot for them to be up there very long. I asked the people to move on and to put their dogs inside their cabins. They were great about it and after half an hour she came down and wandered off with her family.

Bob Schmid pipes up again, his video camera still recording the scene, "I know I must be a nuisance to you guys but I've gotten some marvelous pictures of bears. Last summer my daughter called me outside, 'There's a bear on our dumpster.' A bear was walking around up in the air balancing on the edge of our dumpster, just so graceful."

"Yes," Brad countered, "they are graceful and powerful. Spring of 2000, we had two yearlings wander up from Pennsylvania and they picked up a buddy here. The three of them were out at noon, not just at night, dumping over those big dumpsters. It would take a whole crew of us to set those things back up. These bears had learned to associate people with food. We had to try to teach them that people meant pain. I called the DEC and they sent over their trap. Inside of three weeks we caught all three. We took them over toward Pennsylvania and sent them on their way. The female weighed two-hundred and fifty pounds, the males were both over four hundred."

Bob Sieben raises his hand, is recognized and asks, "Have you seen any injuries?"

"No one hurt. Scared, yes, walking to the john at night and seeing a bear." Brad stopped for a second, and then added, "We did have two close calls last season. A bear climbed into a cabin window while the people were asleep. But they got out OK. Another family was in a pop-up trailer. A bear got up on the picnic table in front of them and was pawing at their screen. We shot the bear with rubber slugs. You see, there are rubber shot and rubber slugs. The shot is for up-close. If you are within 30 yards a slug will go right through a bear." He smiled, "Thirty yards is a good distance for me, too.

"We shot him and he took off flying. I guess the people were out of the Park in the other direction just about as fast. People feed bears and then get mad when they come up on the porch and tear up a cooler.

"Is Mace or pepper spray any good?" someone asks.

"You have to be awful close and if there's any wind, you may get it in your own face. You might just make the bear madder, too. I don't use it. My brother is a State Trooper. He says that in the training to use Mace, they make you experience it. He took the training and said, 'I'd sooner been shot.'

"Bears are fast. The one thing you don't want to do if you are confronted with a bear is to run. Out in Minnesota when we were tracking radio-collared bear on foot we could never catch up to them. Lynn used to track them by air.

"Once Lynn was helping track a wolf pack by air and he found one of his bears. The wolf pack had found her first. She had a den in a pasture. The den was unusual because it had two entrances. There was blood all over the snow. The wolves ate the two cubs but the sow had gotten away. She left two dead wolves. Lynn and the plane arrived over the field just a few minutes after it had happened. The wolves, with blood all over their mouths, were staring up at him.

The room is silent. I am staring far out the window across the lake and into the mountains thinking, *now, that is what you call a Teddy Bear's Picnic. I'm gonna' be careful out there.*

Bob Schmid puts down his video camera and calls for a break. We give Brad a round of applause and Bob leads us over to our own picnic at the table under the trophy buck. The table is piled with banana bread, brownies, cheese strudel and coffee.

Respect Bears

Have you seen one of Allegany's black bears? They're soft and furry looking; really cuddly and cute, aren't they? Almost like the Teddy Bear you had to have in order to go to sleep, right? Wrong! They may look snuggly but they are not. They are wild animals with ferocious teeth and claws and unimaginable strength.

When I was 8 years old back in 1938 my sister and I were at the Buffalo Turnverein Camp, Bee Tee Vee, now called Camp 12, near France Brook Road on the Red House side. In broad daylight a bear came ambling down the road passed the mess hall. I happened to be all alone and I jumped off the porch to follow him. I loved dogs and I guess I thought I could pet this bear. I remember him glancing back over his shoulder at me, his tongue hanging out; me trotting after him. But he had the good sense to pick up the pace and get away from me. I was disappointed. Then a few nights later I started thinking differently about petting bears. We were all sitting at a roaring campfire in the field to the south of the mess hall. It was pitch dark and we had a big, roaring fire with flames and sparks reaching up into the night skies. Andy Lascari, the camp director, was leading us in singing "Old Hiram's Goat" or something, when we heard this awesome crashing and some kind of noise I don't even remember what it was. What I do remember was that someone spotlighted this huge bear. He was on his hind legs with big teeth flashing as he tore the door off our garbage shed, not fifty feet from the campfire.

In the Park years ago, garbage was collected from garbage cans in front of the cabins and deposited in a landfill. Bears made regular rounds of the cans and people gathered at the dump to see them. Sometimes people took their lives in their hands recklessly hand-feeding bears. Some people were hurt. At least one bear had to be destroyed.

In the US and Canada, black bears kill and injure people regularly. When people and bears fraternize; when bears see people as a source of food, people get hurt and bears have to be killed. Do us and the Allegany bears a favor. Enjoy them when you catch a glimpse but keep your distance. Allegany State Park has been relatively lucky so far. Please RESPECT BEARS.

I met a bear hunter on a hike in the Adirondacks once and

when I got home I wrote down what he and I said to each other and what reflections I had then about bears:

Walking the road-like trail to Lake Lila in the Nehasane Preserve I found myself in the company of a stranger. I'll call the stranger Bearhunter.

As I overtook Bearhunter he had an incongruous look about him. He worried along behind him a thing that resembled a shopping cart. He'd stop and swear at it now and again. As I got closer I could see the thing he was pulling was a tiny canoe mounted on wheels. Contained in this vehicle was a shopper's list of what my sometimes too critical eye, saw as disreputable camping gear. So I'm a snob, but I still don't approve of his egg-crate-open-cell foam-rubber mattress.

He was in need of a shave. He wore camouflage coveralls and he talked incessantly. Over his shoulder he carried a worn, bolt-action, thirty-ought-seven rifle. He apologized about the rifle. "My father talked me out of bringing the good gun. I got one that's all engraved and everything. Looks a whole lot better than this one. Don't shoot any better though."

Until then, it had been a dandy September morning. The sky was clear. It was chilly in the sunshine, so a wool shirt felt good. The leaves were just starting to turn. It was green and yellow against flashing blue water and bright sky with once in a while a splash of maple's scarlet.

The quality of the day was the second thing Bearhunter had on his mind. Eventually he said, "Great day, huh?" But way before that came the question, "Have you got some matches? I buried my darn matches down in the pack there somewhere." He had an unlighted cigarette hanging sadly from the corner of his mouth.

The last thing I wanted to do was breathe cigarette smoke out there. I lied and told him, "No."

I immediately felt guilty about that and it got worse because he proved so friendly and such a fountain of information. At first I was just going to dust on past him as quick as I could. He kept on talking so I wasn't able to do that, without offense.

He assured me again that he had matches buried under his load somewhere. "I'd never come out here in the woods for four days without some kind of fire."

He also told me he had just turned forty and had to get away from the family and kids awhile to get used to being that old.

I kind of nodded to him sideways, trying not to trigger any more socialization. Then he dropped the fact that he was going "bear hunting."

My ears perked up at this. It reminded me that this was bear hunting season and I was out in the woods without any bright clothing to protect me from being mistaken for a bear. It also brought vividly to mind an encounter with a mother bear that had started to pursue me the previous month. Besides that, I had just come from Old Forge, where the town was alive with the controversial killing of Old Split Ear, a six-hundred-and-eighty-five pound black bear addicted to the Town garbage dump.

I'd been browsing in the book section of that huge wonderful hardware store in Old Forge. A middle-aged saleslady collared me and lectured half an hour on the life and times of Old Split Ear. Then she sold me Stephen Herrero's excellent book, "Bear Attacks, Their Causes and Avoidance," which scared the wits out of me.

I fell into Bearhunter's pace for the three-mile walk. He had been to Lake Lila forty times, so he said. This was my first. He hunted with bow as well as rifle. He had gotten four deer with his bow over the years and seen a lot of bear while deer hunting. "I've only seen one bear while I was hunting bear though. Never got a shot at one. If I ever killed a bear, one would be enough, I think. I wouldn't have to get any more. Them bear, they come right at you and snap their teeth like they want you to beat it. I'm not going to run this time, if they do it. I'll stand right up to them."

I was wondering what Bearhunter would do with the carcass if he shot even an average-sized three-hundred-pound bear. He was having enough trouble pulling that cart without a bear on top of it. I also wondered if he thought I was being impolite by not offering him a hand with the cart. I prepared myself to argue the point but he was considerate enough not to raise it. I finally managed to break into his rapid stream of monologue by catching him when he inhaled. "Do you hunt bear from a tree stand?" I quickly asked.

"What?" he said. He didn't hear my whole question

because it had come in over some of his last statement. I got half way through repeating my question, and he interrupted laughing. "You shoot a bear in the butt with an arrow and you better be in a tree. A bear can get pretty mad."

He went on to describe the pot of honey and molasses he planned to cook over his fire, "To give them bears some motivation." Of course he didn't stop there. He talked about his family, his hunting, he complained about the lousy wheels on his cart, about the Vermont company that has the contract for the lumber in here and only lets Vermonters drive the road we were hiking, and other things.

When he took his second breath I said, "I ran into a sow and two cubs up in Algonquin Park a month ago and she took off after me." I waited, but he didn't ask me to go on. Instead he started telling me how to improve my hike here at Lake Lila. "You know, I followed these railroad tracks back of the lake. If you go back there a little ways the old railroad station house is still there. It's in great shape but the tracks, look out; they are all tore up. Lots of berry bushes in there, too. Bears love berries. Might see a bear back there. Boy, I love this weather and being out here, don't you?"

I started to say, yup, but he didn't wait that long. He pointed to a rotten log that had been smashed to bits and said, "A bear might have done that, looking for grubs." There were some overturned flat rocks also; indicating them he went on, "Might have been that same bear looking for worms or whatever."

I was catching on to his rules of conversation. Answer your own questions. Don't be a sucker and ask the other guy anything that lets him get into one of his stories. Somehow, when he wasn't paying attention, I slipped in my story about the time I was sleeping in my tent at Lake Colden. A bear bumped me and woke me up as he charged past. He was going for the "bear bag" my neighbor had hung in a nearby tree. Bearhunter had stopped. He looked slyly at me saying, "You ain't supposed to do that."

"Do what?" I said.

"Hang up a bag of food for a bear. It's against the law."

I explained that they weren't baiting the bear; they were just trying to keep their food away from him by hanging it out of reach. But by then, Bearhunter was squatting down at a muddy spot in the road looking at a paw print. "Very big dog or very small bear," he said. It looked like dog to me.

I decided to let him have it with my big bear story. I said, "Couple years ago my wife and I went on a trip up to Churchill, Manitoba to look at polar bears. The guides cooked sardines on the tundra buggy's manifold to bring the bears in."

"That so?" he said. "Friend of mine and I went hunting up at James Bay and we didn't see a thing." Then he was off again. Somewhere along the way he dropped in that New York State has around 4,000 black bears, second only to Pennsylvania and Maine; that 800 bears are harvested in the State each year; that only one in a thousand bear hunters gets a bear. He added, "Bear meat ain't bad if you boil the hell out of it with garlic, black coffee and soda before you roast it. And be sure to put a lot of onions in with it, when you roast it, unless you like the wild taste. I do. I like that wild taste, myself."

So I had to really let him have it. "When I was up in Alaska I got some pictures of grizzlies," I said.
"I never been to Alaska," he replied. "I always wanted to go there."

I figured I had him now. I quick said, "We were visiting Denali Park and I took a joy ride in an airplane to a hunting camp where they were butchering caribou. The pilot was dropping off a guy who claimed he had killed the world record fair-chase polar bear and the skull was in that camp."

"Did you see it?" he asked seeming to break his rule but he was right on.

I answered, "Yes I did," then I had nowhere to go from there. He hung on my last word. His expectant manner demanded a description of that epic chase of which I had only the barest bones. I had already given them to him. So I changed the subject. "What do you think of that Split Ear thing up at Old Forge?"

"Gee, wait till I tell my kids I met someone who's been to Alaska and takes pictures of grizzlies and polar bears," he said. I couldn't quite tell if he was mocking me out or not.

"That Split Ear was quite a big fella, 685 pounds I heard. He might have been a record," I said, shifting about uncomfortably.

"What a waste of an animal," Bearhunter said. "Did you do any hunting up there in Alaska?" he persisted.

I replied truthfully, "No."

"Ever hunt bear around here?"

"No," I answered again. "I only went hunting once in my

life. That was with my dad when I was a kid. We were after woodchucks but we didn't see anything so we shot at some tin cans."

"Tin cans," he said with some kind of questioning look. It pleased me when he dropped the subject of my exploits and finally picked up the bait on Old Forge's problem. "People were making a regular circus out of those bears in Old Forge. They closed down the dump two years ago. Twenty or thirty bears had been making a living out of that dump. Then they'd sit on their front porches, stick honey all over their feet and let Old Split Ear come and lick it off. Then someone decides Split Ear's getting to be a nuisance and they gut shoot him and let him rot in the woods. What a crying waste."

"Did you see all the letters in the Adirondack Express arguing about it?" I asked.

"Yes, I saw them letters and I agree with every one of them. There's two sides to every story. I can see how the guy who shot that bear was worried about his kids and ticked off about the bear waking up the dogs every night. I can see how that guy's mother would come out to back him up the way she did. After all it was her kid. And I can see how all the people who liked to feed Split Ear got a kick out of him. I just don't see how them folks could be so stupid as to go on feeding bears in town and not realize the mess they were getting into. You feed bears and bears are going to come to your house to eat."

"I guess the Department of Environmental Conservation tried to help," I commented.

"Well, yes and no," he laughed. "They tried to drive Split Ear off with rubber bullets and cayenne pepper spray and air horns but that never did any good. They even carried him away over into the Moose River Wilderness. But tell me they didn't know he'd be back. They knew that wasn't far enough. He came back next spring and got shot down like a dog. It wasn't no hunting, no sport, just murder."

By then we had reached the lake. A party with a very big dog occupied the lean-to there. I thought Bearhunter would come along with me and bend their ears too but he stood firmly on the trail. "Aren't you going to say hello?" I asked.

"Nope, I'll say good-bye here. I don't like the look of that big dog." We shook hands and parted company.

I visited at the lean-to, praised their catch of fish and patted their dog. Then I went on down the road another mile or so and found a log to sit on for lunch. I was thinking about bears and people. I thought of that poor little squirt, Bearhunter, sitting out in the woods, all alone, boiling a pot of honey and molasses. Maybe he'd attract a bear and kill it. Maybe the bear would make a meal out of Bearhunter. The odds seemed fairer out in the woods than those did that greeted poor Old Split Ear in town. Split Ear must have been so surprised when one of those nice people who left out garbage for him let him have it, in the guts, with a shotgun.

My unconscious did a funny trick then. It dragged up the image of Goldilocks marauding through the house of the three bears and of their mild reaction. "Somebody's been eating my porridge and they ate it all up." What a contrast, to Old Split Ear's treatment.

Stephen Herrero's Bear Attack book was fresh in my mind. Herrero says black bears are timid in comparison to grizzlies and yet in the US and Canada between 1960 and 1980 there were 500 black bear attacks on people. He knew of 23 fatalities. In 1978, three boys went fishing in Algonquin Park and were killed by a black bear. In 1990, two adults were killed by a black bear on Lake Opeongo. I wasn't far from there this summer when I met that mama bear picking berries. And she took offense.

Sitting there on the shores of beautiful Lake Lila peacefully eating my lunch, I heard a rustling in the brush. I took a cautious look around and saw nothing. Then there was a distinct odor of fish in the air, which I hadn't noticed before. I thought, oh, oh, bear breath. I thought I heard something more in the bushes. I picked up my lunch and put it in my pack. I walked straight back to the road and went for home. I don't know if there was a bear sniffing around me there at Lake Lila or if Bearhunter was trying to scare me or if it was my nerves chewing on a lot of bear data. I know a bear didn't eat me. I didn't even see one.

I like to think though that it was Old Split Ear's ghost looking for a handout. But I was careful not to leave anything for him to eat, or for any of his cousins, lest they get the wrong idea about the possibility of being friends with people and get themselves or some of us killed.

Another
Big Surprise Down in the Woods

(Brad Whitcomb, the newly appointed Park Forester, spoke to the Allegany State Park Historical Society on the subject of animals in the Park at our April 17th, 2002 meeting. I interviewed him afterward. Then I picked out all the bear stories and put them together into "A Big Surprise Down in the Woods." But there was so much good stuff about other Park critters that I had to write this second chapter.)

Here's the scene: The Allegany State Park Historical Society is gathered in the main hall on the first floor of the Red House Administration Building. Forester Brad Whitcomb describes a bloody encounter out in Minnesota, viewed from the air; a mother bear has just killed two wolves and escapes with her life but is unsuccessful in defending her two cubs against the rest of the wolf pack.

Brad leaves us in awe and me with the resolve to temper my love of wild creatures with plenty of caution.

In ten minutes we reconvene. Brad drags out a four-foot-square, hollow wooden frame, made of two-by-eights. Its open face is covered by galvanized wire mesh with half-inch openings. I've got no idea what this is about and by their expressions, I don't think anyone else in the audience has either.

Brad explains, "This is a platform for the nest that a pair of osprey has built on a Niagara Mohawk power pole. It's the corner pole, to your left, as you come in the Red House entrance, off '86.'" He's back at his stride, telling us about osprey, the big fish-eating hawks that are reestablishing themselves in the Park.

"The nest is very close to high voltage lines. A wet stick across two lines could cause a nasty fire. So we are going to move the osprey. We will have to shut down all the power to the Park for ten or fifteen minutes. The move is a big cooperative effort that involves Ni-Mo (Niagara Mohawk Power Company), the DEC

(NYS Department of Environmental Conservation), the Corps (US Army Corps of Engineers), OPRHP, (NYS Office of Parks and Historic Preservation) and the Seneca Nation.

"The Corps has to issue a permit for the operation because the pole is in a pond, a flooded wetland that we will have to drain. They also handle the bird banding to keep track of the birds. It's a Ni-Mo pole so they do the actual job. Ni-Mo is also providing training for the Corps' bird bander so he can work around hot wires. The Senecas will be there with their ambulance crew, in case anyone gets hurt. I'll be there for the Park and the birds.

"The new pole has to be taller than the old one. Osprey like to be high. They won't go to a lower pole.

"You can't pick up an osprey nest like an ordinary bird's nest. It's made of sticks and would fall apart. Ni-Mo's guy takes a special contraption up there using one of those cherry-picker-bucket-trucks. It is a couple of pieces of plywood that he slides under the nest from either side and then bolts together. Then he can hoist the whole nest all in one piece."

Turning to the nesting platform, Brad said, "We are mounting this new one on the side of the pole. Makes it much more convenient for the guy who has to climb up there to band the birds." He stops to smile at the impossibility of the image which he is about to create for us. "It's tough reaching up over the edge of the platform and into the nest if the platform sits right on top of the pole."

Someone in the audience asks, "Don't the mom-and-pop-birds get aggravated when you're messing with their nest?"

Brad sticks his hands in his pockets like that isn't part of his job or, if it is, it isn't the part he likes best and he nods, "Yes, they do. They come buzzing at you. The guy who does that work says, 'You just don't pay any attention to them. You might get hit with a wing once in a while.'

"He goes up there with a perforated pail and lowers the chicks to put bands on them down on the ground. Two years ago this pair had a pretty good year. They hatched out three eggs. Last year for some reason they only laid one egg and it didn't hatch. The Corps looks at the eggs that don't produce. They try to work out why. Maybe weather, not enough food or maybe pesticides. The water's been low in the Kinzua Reservoir but that's good for the birds. Think how much safer a fish feels with eight foot of water over top of him rather than just two or three foot.

"Altogether we've got three osprey nests. There is one in Kane Hollow, the one at the Red House entrance, we've been talking about and one over in Quaker on '280,' all of them on power poles. The one on '280,' we didn't have to move the nest. We were able to lower the wires around it."

Brad slides the nesting platform towards us and turns it around, running the palm of his hand over the wire mesh, "The mesh lets bird droppings fall to the ground instead of fouling up the nest. Looking at what they drop you can see that they eat mainly suckers and carp. I do remember one time. We had just finished stocking trout into Quaker Lake and I saw this big old osprey flying off with a 'brooky' to take home to the kiddies."

Bob Sweet boomed from the audience with the distinct glee of what sounded to me like an old fish poacher, "Did he say, 'Thank you?'"

Brad grinned, "No, but he looked happy. That fish couldn't have been in the water five minutes."

He added, "Osprey go south in the winter, for better fishing. We get Trumpeter Swans and Tundra Swans come through here just as the ice is going out. Hard to tell those swans apart. They're both big white birds. We don't have a resident population of loons here, but transients stop off. I heard them out there last night." And in our imaginations we all recalled the lonely hoot of the loon.

Bob Schmid, still taking pictures with his video camera, broke in, "Have you seen bobcats?"

Brad answered, "No, I haven't. I understand a Seneca shot two, not long ago. The cats had just killed a turkey."

Bob came back with, "I heard someone say, they saw seven coyotes hunting in a pack."

Brad said, "I've never seen more than one coyote at a time. They are usually solo hunters. We don't have wolves around here but out in Minnesota I've seen them hunting in packs. It's almost like they sit down and make up a plan first. Joe France told me he was out turkey hunting and found a den of coyotes."

Terry Perkins a, retired Forest Ranger, had been listening attentively. He speaks up. "In 2000, I saw a river otter over in Wolf

Run, gorgeous thing. Must have been one of those that the DEC released."

"Never saw a river otter," Brad admits ruefully.

Bob says, "How come there's so many foxes around. I've been seeing a lot of foxes lately."

Brad says, "Foxes are cyclical, like a lot of animals. Depends on the rabbits, if there are a lot of rabbits, then you see a lot of fox. When there's not enough food, disease takes over. They become more susceptible to things like rabies."

He stopped and then said with special emphasis, "We have never had any animal in the Park test positive for rabies.

"Couple years ago, I was up in my office here in this building. Someone come running in said, 'They got a deer out in the parking lot.' I went down. Six or eight people were standing around petting a doe. One guy was feeding her.

Brad shakes his head saying, "I'm worried about them. I'm thinking rabies, and wondering what else it might be they were getting into with her. Something was wrong. They found her standing by the road. One of them had walked right up to her and she didn't move. They picked her up, put her in the back of a truck and drove her here. We sent her over to the DEC to be examined.

He took a deep breath that seemed to express relief at being safely out of that encounter between deer and people. Then he went on, "Deer are usually lightning fast. They're a lot of work to catch. We got together on a program with the DEC in February of '98, '99 and 2000. We radio collared thirty-six deer trying to learn their winter feeding grounds, where they go in the summer, how far they range and how long they survive.

"The bucks have a pretty wide range. Wherever you catch them they'll take off and find the way back to their home. The does never go far. A lot of them stay near Camp Allegany and over by Camp 12.

We collared mostly does. The neck on a buck swells, during the rut, and the DEC only had a few of the special collars to use for them.

"There's a cider mill that supplies us with what's left of the apples after they're done squeezing them. We put it out in a bait box in a pasture and let the deer get used to eating there. Then we set up rocket-powered net traps. Deer are awful fast. They have to have their heads right down inside the bait box when the rockets go off or they get away. They out run the rockets.

"Usually, when it works, we catch two or three. Our record is five. They are thrashing around tangled under the net. We have to wrestle them down and give them injections of tranquilizers with hypodermic syringes. We have bales of hay around as camouflage. While the deer are unconscious we cover them up with loose hay to keep 'em warm. For some reason, you can't give them the antidote for an hour. We stay around with them till we know that they're OK, no coyote got at them or anything.

"Hunter told me once that he shot a deer in the Park. He went back to pick up his buddy at the Summit Cabins to help him carry it out. By the time they got back to the deer, twenty minutes or so later, the deer had been half eaten by coyotes. The coyotes were long gone.

"Coyotes are fast and don't like people. Someone caught one on film. He was charging down-hill like a freight train after a deer and crossed a concealed trap line. He smelled human and stopped dead. Turned around and shot back up that hill like a rocket.

"In '98 we collared nine deer. Two were button bucks. We gave them all names. Alex, we found his collar cut off over in Sunfish. If the collar doesn't move for some time it sends what they call a mortality signal and we go find it. Jennifer, we lost track of. Then we got a call from North Warren PA. She'd been seen around there, with her collar on, for a year and then an archer shot her. Of the nine, two were road kills, three were killed by hunters, one we aren't sure of and three are alive and well today. The one they named after me got shot right away."

To me, Brad's stories say: Wild animals live an amazing, precarious life in the woods. The balance is narrow between prey and predator. Man, as a top predator, has responsibility for the others but is at risk, too.

Deer Overpopulation
And DEC Deer Management
1995

Most of us find them beautiful to watch. Some value them as venison. However we feel about deer, there are too many of them in Allegany State Park and they are eating her forests out of house and home. The Department of Environmental Conservation counts 30 deer per square mile there. Foresters say that with any more than 15 deer per square mile a mature forest cannot regenerate.

Deer enjoying Red House bird feeder

Allegany is unique for its forest of big trees over 80, some over 350, years old. Deer grazing and the dense sun-limiting canopy of the mature forest limit growth on the forest floor. That means few young replacement trees and not enough cover for songbirds and small mammals like possum and porcupine.

In earlier times natural conditions, including predators like wolves and panthers, culled the deer herd and the forest thrived. The DEC now manages herd size through the number of hunting permits and it issues too few to do the job.

In 1994 hunters took 917 of the 3000 deer in the park. Female deer over a year old produce twins each year. The herd easily replaces its loss. The forest can't catch up.

The problem lies in the way the DEC decides how many deer hunting permits to issue. It is left in the hands of the hunters. The Park is one of 99 Deer Management Units in the State. Every five years, the DEC names a task force for each unit with people who are interested in deer, mostly hunters. The task force meets twice to form a consensus as to size of the deer herd desired. DEC increases or decreases the number of hunting permits to reach that size.

I am a member of the Park task force. At the end of February, DEC rangers gave us an orientation on deer management. We met again a month later. There was only one other non-deer hunter in the group and she didn't come to the second meeting. Almost everybody seemed to conclude that there were not enough deer in the Park and that we should issue fewer hunting permits and let the herd increase.

The State forester for the Park got up and said, "Fellas, there are too many deer in the Park. We need a 20% decrease. Let's give the forest a chance."

Two of us backed him up. The others compromised. Instead of the initially proposed 50% increase in Park deer, they settled for a 15% increase. They were not impressed with what this would do to the forest. I abstained from the final vote in protest.

After the meeting I said to the ranger in charge, "Hunters are less than 2% of the million and a half people who come to the Park each year. How come you don't ask the rest for their opinions?"

He said, "You wouldn't like what that 98% would say either. They want to see deer."

The State forester jumped in, "It depends on how you ask the question. If they knew that the price of this big deer herd is that the woods get ruined and they don't get to see any other wildlife but deer, you'd get a different answer."

I headed home in the dark. At the first cross road, just over the Red House dam, what do you think my headlights picked up? Right! Grazing at the side of the road were 20 scrawny deer.

DEC Deer Management 2000

The DEC Deer Management Unit for Allegany State Park met again after five years to decide the next five year goal for the size of the Park deer herd.

DEC now estimated there were 2700 deer in the park, 27 per square mile, down from the 30 per square mile of 5 years ago. The apparent decrease was probably not significant since it was within the range of error of the system they used to make the estimate. About 500 deer are taken by hunters each year. That leaves roughly 20 to 22 deer per square mile after the culling. Terry Dailey, the Park forester, told us he thought the right size would be more like 19.

Rick White, the naturalist from the Pfeiffer Nature center near Porterville and a frequenter of the Park, felt that the herd needed to be cut more severely. He related the lack of under story to both too many deer and the lack of any logging. He felt that badly restricts habitat for several species of migratory birds, some of which were in danger of extinction.

DEC representatives leaned in the direction of a smaller herd because Allegany deer are chronically short of food and therefore small and not very attractive to hunters.

Listening to this I formed the view that the Park had too many deer and was overgrazed. I thought we should authorize the harvesting of a larger number of deer. There was no other practical way to control the size of the deer herd. Deer continued to dominate the flora and fauna of the Park. We had a lot more of them around than Columbus did when he got over here.

Task force members were armed with the questionnaire below and asked to interview our friends with it and report back.

NEW YORK STATE DEER MANAGEMENT UNIT

CITIZEN TASK FORCE

Worksheet for Collecting Stakeholder Opinions

Please state briefly; in the space that follows, why you consider yourself a stakeholder in the issue of the size of the deer herd in Allegany State Park...

Below please mark your option with an x

In your opinion is this year's deer herd in Allegany State Park:
Increasing
decreasing
stable
don't know

In your opinion, is this year's herd there:
too high
too low
about right
don't know

Over the next 5 years do you think the deer herd should:
increase by   %
decrease by   %
remain stable
don't know

What reason do you have for your last answer?

Responses to the Questionnaire

I talked with 15 people who had an interest in Allegany State Park. They did not all follow the neat DEC outlines but they did all express relevant opinions.

There was only one person with a really different opinion. He felt that we ought to take a careful look at the Animal Rights approach to deer control before we seconded the DEC hunting approach.

Everyone else felt that overgrazing of the Allegany's forest under story was throwing off the natural balance of flora and fauna and indicated a need for culling the deer herd further than in the past. The recommended levels ran from 10 to 19 deer per square mile.

A few found hunting not to their liking but recognized that it was the only alternative. Some felt that the problem was quite acute and extreme. Adding up their opinions, I reported that my group favored 12 to 15 deer per square mile.

This number of deer in the Park would allow the forest to recover. It would make the sighting of a deer more unusual and a thing to be sought after rather than a nuisance. It would also allow deer sufficient nutrients to grow to a healthy size.

The task force wound up recommending a 20% cut in the herd to 16-18 deer per square mile.

Allegheny Uprising
Memorial Day 2001

The whole shebang was to wind up in a "Public Outreach Event" to draw attention to the outrageous "East Side Timber Sale." That sale was to be the largest National Forest timber sale ever in the Eastern United States. 8571 acres of Pennsylvania's 500, 000 acre Allegheny National Forest was up for clear-cutting. "Heartwood" put this protest together. It is an association dedicated to the health and well-being of the central hardwood forests of the United States.

George Heron, twice president of the Seneca Nation, gave the opening address. He made a severe indictment of the federal government for building the Kinzua Dam and flooding the Seneca Allegany Reservation just north of the Allegheny National Forest. The ANF itself is now threatened by the National Forest Service policy of managing forests, primarily for timber harvest. That policy both loses money and sacrifices mature forests, forests that you and I, the citizens of the United States, own.

Pennsylvania's Allegheny Defense Project hosted this year's Heartwood Council May 25 to 28 in the Allegheny National Forest. I was privileged to enjoy a delicious one-day taste of the meeting. A hundred or so of us gathered in a woodsy campground. There were primitive sleeping camps and a mess hall with a giant fireplace. Mornings, after breakfast, expert panels convened the group in the meadow to debate and inform on the forest-threatening issues: oil and gas exploration, ATVs and logging as well as strategies to protect against those threats. Afternoons were trips into the woods: for looking at the damage clear-cutting and herbicides had done, for appreciating the wonderful forest that remains and for hands-on experience in techniques of defending the forest.

So, there we were, at Hickory Creek in the midst of the ANF. The sun blinking around lumps of cumulus left from a morning's shower twinkled on our rock strewn, 30-foot-wide stream. The forest floor along its banks was strewn in ferns. Here and there patches of wildflowers preened where sunshine penetrated the fresh green over story of beech, maple and black cherry. The air was damp and fragrant of pine and moss. Then, with a merry splash, Ann Phillippi, our instructor, sneakers, dungarees and all, jumped into the creek in a foot-deep spot. In her big voice this ruddy-faced sturdy woman yelled at us, "Y'all come on in, the water's hot."

I followed her. After all, I thought, she's a zoology professor and she's leading our afternoon workshop. She knows what she's doing.

The water was, distinctly, not hot, but the teaching was.

Ann Phillippi's chilling, hands-on and feet-in workshop at Hickory Creek Recreation Area was a "bash". She had the 12 of us turning over rocks, seining with a huge net and scooping with tiny ones. We gently dumped our finds, "critters," as she called them, into shallow white basins as she called out their names and detailed their significance. "That's a Stone Fly. Look at him pulsate. He must be doing something territorial. He's worried about that other one. See the dark spots on his back? His wings are starting there.

These guys are predators. They eat everything: that Caddis fly, that May fly."

Frankly the ugly twin-tailed, big-jawed bully of a bug didn't look anything like a fly to me. But Ann told us about the five larval stages they go through in one to three years. Each of those times they shed their skin. In the dramatic final transformation, they emerge as a winged ephemeral, live for a single day of procreation, then die, presumably in ecstasy.

What's the point of all this on a forest preservation outing? Ann explained the point, "If you can testify as to what life you found in a stream above a logging operation and what you found below, your scientific precision in identifying the damage to the ecology of the stream will be impressive. If you know what kind of life there should be in a first, second or third order stream and you compare it with what is actually there you will have convincing testimony on the health of the stream."

Of course Ann had to explain to us, uninitiated, that a second order stream, like Hickory Creek which engulfed us to our knees, occurs when two first order streams merge. A first order stream is the smallest of those marked on a US Geological Survey Quadrangle. On average a first order stream runs for about a mile. A third order stream results when two second-orders come together. The Nile and the Mississippi are 10th order. "Each order has its characteristic critters," she said.

Ann's 11-year-old son and one of his buddies enthusiastically spilled a six-inch minnow out of their net into a pan. "Hey thanks", Ann exclaimed as she carefully added enough water for the minnow to swim. "That's a Dace. Y'all are privileged to see, let me see," she thumbed through a well-worn manual. "I believe that is a Red-Sided Dace, unless it is a Blunt-nosed Dace. Anyway these Dace only live in first and second order streams. That means this is a pretty healthy crick. And all those crayfish mean there's plenty of life here. They eat all the dead stuff so we know there's plenty of life" (we had put six crabs in the pans; someone counted 26 under one rock.).

We had five minnows in the pan when we found one that looked different. Ann said, "See how he has two fins on his ventral side instead of just one like we think a normal fish should have.

That's a Darter. He uses those like arms to rest on the bottom and to stir up food."

I was learning. I had always thought a minnow was just a baby fish. In fact minnows are a species of fish most of which are small. Baby fish are known as "fry" like in "small fry."

"Look what I got," yelled a hulk of a gray-bearded man in shorts and knee-high waders as he splashed gleefully up to the group. His big fist was closed and when he passed its contents into Ann's grasp a frog displayed his head and two legs between her fingers. "Look-a-here will you," she exclaimed. "Well thank you. Look-a-here, at the mask. Y'all really are privileged. This is a Wood Frog. You don't see many of these. This is a healthy stream." She offered Mr. Wood Frog to me. I let the young lady next to me take it. I've had warts enough, though I understand that frogs are in more danger from our microbes than we are from theirs.

Ann spoke for a few moments and summarized why we were all there. "They say the leaves that fall in these first order streams drive life on the planet earth. They feed the oceans. When they fall, they are covered with fish food, that slick frosting of mold and bacteria. All this flows down the succession of streams. The critters in the stream store the energy flowing down. Saving a forest saves this system of energy collection and storage. It saves life."

I had only the one day so I made do with the fun and information Ann had provided. That Public Outreach event to draw attention to the "East Side Timber Sale" sounded desperately important and like fun too, but I did not attend. I'm making up for it by writing this.

Heartwood is leading an "uprising" to take back our State and National Forests for us to enjoy them and for our grand kids to enjoy them too.

Osgood Trail Assessment, December 8, 2002

On this snowshoe climb of the Osgood Trail there was seven to ten inches of snow on the ground. The wind was blowing hard off and on. Sometimes the sky was densely overcast, almost black, and snow fell heavily on us. Then the clouds opened up, the snow halted and brilliant sun lit the woods.

The Osgood Trail is off Macintosh Cabin Trail very near Allegany State Park Highway 2. It is well-marked with a large glassed-in map. The trail head parking area was plowed clear of snow. Deer tracks were evident and proved to be a reliable guide to the trail.

We followed the deer and the trail markers a few hundred yards in where we came upon an old road bed that crosses the trail. Confusingly, there is a trail marker that suggests this road is a hiking trial. That marker should be removed.

The woods are pleasingly dense. There is a plantation of red pine, but then mostly deciduous trees including some big black cherry. There are only a few small white pines.

A short distance beyond that crossing road a doe, that had lain in the snow till we were passed her, startled us. She darted along parallel to us and off up the hill. Another most pleasing aspect of the trail is all the boulders. Osgood Trail is a miniature Thunder Rock.

We hiked the looping trail from its base at 1460 feet and, according to our instruments, topping out at 2180. In route we found only one significant blow-down, a dandy, on the northwestern side of the loop, not far from the union with the main trail. That blowdown should go.

Checking Osgood Trail map

There is a clearing at the top of the trail. There the weather broke and treated us to a view of distant mountains. For lunch, we escaped the wind by sitting down behind a primitive shelter of branches. We thanked the survival class that put it together for us.

Continuing the loop and gliding down off the top on our snowshoes was delightful. We followed an at-first obvious path between the trees. Abruptly it disappeared and we found ourselves in woods with hardly a clue which way to go. We followed deer tracks and ancient graffiti carved in trees like, "Joey loves Melissa," illustrated with a heart. For a long stretch there were very few trail marking disks and none easy to find. There may be a path in the forest floor but it is not useful with ten inches of snow on top of it.

When we crossed our inbound tracks, we discovered that on the way up we had breezed right passed the marker for this return loop. If the junction was easier to find you could take your pick of approaches to the summit to take.   Better marking, in general, is called for on this northwestern side of the loop.

We finished the 2.5 mile trip in 2.5 hours. Coming down was more fun than the steamy up-hill trip. As our hostess, the doe, scampered past in farewell, we thought, it's a crying shame that more of life isn't a downhill, as pretty as this one.

Beehunter Trail
Work Party and Chili Fest
May 4, 1997

The weather forecast was for rain. Ten of us of us, led by Walter Meyer, turned out in ponchos and Gortex and we were blessed. The sun came out, the sky was blue. It was more like summer than spring and the bugs never caught on. The forest floor was covered with little purple spring beauties, and lush full leafed greens that we named swamp lilies. We had gotten there ahead of leaf-out and were treated to distant vistas that we do not usually see from Beehunter.

A widow-maker we left for the experts

We attacked considerable blowdown with a big crosscut saw and thereby proved and disproved several manhoods and womanhoods. Some of us delighted in mucking-out waterbars while other specialized in lopping back raspberry bushes.

When we completed the 6.5 mile circuit Walter Meyer treated us to a   4 o'clock dinner centering on his judiciously seasoned, delicious chili. There is more to be done. We will be going again soon.

North Country Trail Assessment
ASP 3 to ASP 1
August 31, 2002.

We walked this trail section from noon to about 4pm on a beautiful summer Saturday. Generally we found the trail in fair condition.

There were a total of 21 significant blowdowns obstructing the path. They ranged from tops of trees totally obstructing the pathway and forcing extensive detours to 10-inch trunks that could be easily stepped over. Some of these might be left in place to discourage vehicular travel. Many should be removed.

Blowdown

The trail has been relocated at both its ends in recent years and the large map-containing signs marking the trail heads should be moved accordingly. The materials in the map case on ASP 3 are in very bad shape. The case itself on ASP 1 has been damaged by missiles of some sort.

It is not clear from the maps or the trail markings whether Horse Trail 17 and Foot Trail 9 (North Country) share the same right of way where Trail 9 leaves ASP 1. There is a mud hole made by horse traffic in this area.

Several sections of trail have been improved by wooden walkways. There are a few more spots that could use this treatment, notably one at altitude 2020 feet. There are a few overgrown sections of trail where it is difficult to find your way through brush. One of these is at about 2.6 miles from ASP 1.

At one spot a hard-working crew has placed a number of boulders in a stream that make for easy fording and allows the stream to flow by well.

We were pleased to find the relatively new lean-to at 2.1 miles with its picnic table where we stopped for lunch. But we were disappointed to see that raccoons or porcupines are attracted to the material coating the log walls of the lean-to and have eaten much of them away. In one spot they have opened a hole to the rear. The outhouse is in good condition but needs a new seat.

Older of two lean-tos on the Stony Book Trail

There is a second older lean-to nearby whose log walls are in better condition than the new one. However, the roof on this one needs work. Someone has tacked a messy old poncho over the lean-to's open face and there are cans and bottles in its fire pit.

At about 3.5 miles from ASP 1 or 1 mile form ASP 3 there are orange ribbons that seem to mark an illegal trail running off of trail 9.

The beaver pond about half way is an attractive spot. There are huge black cherry trees and ancient hemlock groves and some wild rocky places and views down into Stony Creek that add up to a remarkable hike.

Summit Fire Tower Restoration

Anastasia Flannigan Gray

"The embers danced out ahead of the fire, 1/4, 1/2, 3/4 mile, and started new fires. Burning debris rolled down rock faces and set vegetation afire farther down. ...I was sure nothing would be left when I returned except the steel of the tower..." That's not Allegany State Park. That's Sequoia National Forest, California. Carol Ann Ralston, a Forest Fire Observer, was describing the view from her fire tower there on July 22, 2000. Here in the Northeast, fires like that are rare but not women Fire Observers. One of Allegany's best known Forest Fire Observers was a woman, Anastasia Flannigan Gray.

Allegany State Park's last big fire was around 1900, before it was even a Park. Then over a thousand acres of slash, left by logging operations, burned along Dry Creek. That area stands out now, north of Allegany State Park Highway 3 just east of Science Lake; the fire killed the beech and maple so black cherry dominates.

In the 1920's the Park constructed three steel fire observation towers: one on South Mountain overlooking Salamanca and the valley of the Allegany River, a second near the Bradford entrance to the Park and a third on Mount Tuscarora South of Quaker Run Headquarters. The Bradford tower is gone. The other two are in need of repair.

These towers were a part of a system of towers across New York State organized by the Department of Environmental Conservation to detect and control forest fires. The DEC stationed observers in them with maps and radios. When they observed signs of fire, they radioed the compass direction to headquarters, where they pinpointed the fire by plotting directions from three towers. In those days of less efficient communications, tower observers, using their radios, arranged the delivery of men and fire-fighting equipment to the fire site.

In the 1970's fire towers became obsolete. "Their job was taken over by airplane observation and radios," said Region 9 DEC Forester, Dan Richter, of Olean. He's the one in charge of forest fire prevention and control. "But we don't use planes anymore. The last flights were in the '80's. Technology has changed. Radios are so much better, we have Global Positioning Satellites, everyone has a cell phone and all the local fire companies are well trained.

216

They have brushfire trucks that can get in almost anywhere."
Ranger Richter closed with, "A lot of observers were women."

Summit Fire Tower

Which brings us back to Anastasia Gray and her
granddaughter, Mary Jones, who remembered that "Fire Warden
Grandmother of hers." Mary Jones is an academic dean at Dubois
College in Pennsylvania and a former Salamanca resident.

"We all adored her. Everyone loved her. She knew the job
was important. People were friendly, the living was easy, and she
was a social person. Up the tower all day, down for lunch, happy,
cheerful, laughed at her own expense." Anastasia, according to her

granddaughter, was "always sociable and pretty when she was young. She belonged to everything. And I think that's what made her so good at her job. She loved all those visitors who climbed the tower every year."

Anastasia's main job in life was mother and homemaker. Her husband, Harry Gray, worked for the Railroad until the middle 1930's. Then he took the Forest Fire Observer job and manned Summit Tower for Allegany State Park. W.W.II had made men scarce when, in 1943, a heart attack took him suddenly. Anastasia knew the job; the family needed the income, so she took it over for the next dozen years.

"She had long gray hair that I used to love to brush for her," Mary said. "She braided and twisted it into a coil on top of her head. She was five-foot-four, pleasingly plump and always wore a housedress. She put an apron on when she was cooking. I never saw her in jeans or slacks. She was a very feminine woman but could split her own stove wood and pump her own water."

"There was a cabin up there behind the tower. In early spring and late fall when it was cold she commuted from Salamanca but most of the summer she lived up there, alone. She never was afraid. Of course, she had her shotgun. My cousins and I used to love to go up there and stay with her. We'd pick strawberries and hike and swim. We had to bring water in bottles; there wasn't any electricity, just kerosene lamps. We'd play games till dark and then go to bed."

"Bears used to come around the cabin when they could smell bacon frying or something. Gramma showed us how to beat on a pan rhythmically to scare them off. When she was gone-off a few times they'd break in the screen on the back porch. Sometimes we would hear porcupines chewing real loud on the supports for the cabin. We were horrified when our nice grandma went out there and shot off her shotgun. She'd come back in saying 'Oh, I just scared the "porky" away.' One time we found a dead one she had shot."

"I remember once we were playing on the steps of the tower. Gramma was up in the cabin on top of it and couldn't see. A bear came out of the woods and started up the stairs. We were dodging from platform to platform and encouraging him, 'Here bear, here bear, come here nice bear.' She got a little upset about that."

"She never had to deal with any major fires in the Park but there were often fires along the river on the Seneca Reservation. Up in the tower, she had a round table with a map on it covered with glass. She didn't use any instruments. She'd just eyeball the location and then phone it in. I remember the phone with a crank on it hanging on the wall in the cabin"

The day the Beahan family climbed the Tuscarora Tower

The spring and fall are the fire seasons. But Mary said her grandmother was much busier in the summer when long lines of campers would climb the tower to enjoy the view with her. Anastasia had them sign her books and she'd have 800 to a thousand signatures a year. "People came from all over the country and the world and she exchanged Christmas cards with many of them."

"Gramma used to sing nursery rhymes to the little kids so they would dance. She told stories to the kids. She explained Park history to their parents. She was a tour guide. She never met anyone she didn't like. Any girl would aspire to be like her."

Over the phone Mary Jones herself sounded, to me, a lot like Anastasia Flannigan Gray, her grandmother and Allegany State Park Summit Tower Fire Warden extraordinaire.

We must say a prayer and be thankful that Allegany State Park's fire towers have been known for the hearty, warm hospitality of Fire Wardens like Anastasia and Harry Gray and their successors, Francis Bousquet and Fritz Opferbeck, and not for the battling of fire-storm.

Fire Tower
Pat McGee to the Rescue

Allegany State Park Historical Society
ASP Route 1, Suite 3
Salamanca NY14379-9753

Dear Senator McGee,

The Allegany State Park Historical Society and the Adirondack Mountain Club have been working on a project that we hope you have heard about and which we think may be close to your heart.

You must remember and must have climbed some of the old fire towers in the Park. Most of us have. But that experience is not open to our grand kids. The two towers that remain in the Park, one on Mountain Tuscarora and the other near the Summit aren't in good enough repair to let folks up them.

We have formed a committee of members from both clubs and quite a number of other people who are just interested. This Fire Tower Restoration Committee has had the Summit tower surveyed and it will cost about $60,000 to put it back in shape.

We have gotten contributions from both club treasuries with which we put together a brochure advertising our restoration project. We have sent out a mailing to volunteer fire companies and to businesses asking for contributions. We have designed a Fire Tower patch that our members have been busy selling at Park functions, at their meetings and at anybody else's meetings who would let us in. In this way we have raised a few thousand dollars.

Most of these funds are being used to build a kiosk near the Summit Tower that will interpret its history to hikers. The remainder will be used to try to develop more funds.

The Tower will be fun. It will provide another opportunity for the Park's great forest to be explained and appreciated. It will increase the value of a visit to the Park to all who go there.

Now here is the problem: We have been working hard at this and the money is just not coming in so that we can expect to see this dream fulfilled in any reasonable time. We believe New York State tax dollars are needed and deserved.

Please consider requesting a Member Item of $60,000 to complete the restoration of the Summit Fire Tower.

The Allegany State Park Historical Society is incorporated, able and willing to handle these monies.

Sincerely

Bob Schmid
President, Allegany State Park Historical Society

Enclosed:
Fire Tower Restoration Brochure and Fire Tower Commemorative Patch

CC:
George Wyman
Mike Miecznikowski

An Invitation

Allegany State Park Fire Tower Dedication
12 Noon Saturday June 1, 2002
At the Foot of the Summit Fire Tower

From: Allegany State Park Fire Tower Restoration Committee

To: Everyone interested in restoring the Allegany State Park Summit Fire Tower

YOU ARE INVITED

Help us celebrate. We have built a wood and stone kiosk at the base of the old Summit Fire Tower. Panels that tell the story of the tower are waiting in the Park, completed. NYS Parks Department, Historic Preservation people did themselves proud in making them. Our committee provided the information and raised the funds. We will install the panels in time for our dedication ceremonies scheduled for Saturday June 1st at 1PM.

There will be a tent, hot dogs and drinks for lunch and Terry Dailey has promised to bring along some other old timers to swap fire tower stories with us.

We are inviting Commissioner Castro and a few other dignitaries to help mark the occasion.

The whole party should last about an hour.

Remember: On June 1st, 2002, at 12 Noon, right in the shadow of our tower, we will meet for the dedication.

Come along, bring the kids, have lunch and celebrate!

Trip to New Ireland

*If you should be tempted to visit New Ireland remember,
"Take nothing but pictures; leave nothing but footprints. Leave the
relics there for all to see, else the divil will come and take ye."*

Paul Lewis promised to take us to New Ireland. That's
Allegany State Park's bygone village of Irish immigrants. He and
his history class at Cleveland Hill High School have made a prize-
winning study of it, so he knows the place well. It was a beautiful
sunny May Day in the Park, as we sat confined indoors at the Red
House Administration building. Paul seemed to be Welshing on the
deal. "It's been raining for a week and there's going to be lots of
mud and bugs up there," said he, this squarely-built man in the
longish black crew cut and bristling black moustache. He was at
ease before us in the casual manner of the longtime teacher and
athletic coach that he is.

He says, "Now, for the good of the Order, we have to
decide what we're gonna do." That "for the good of the Order"
interested me. I asked him later and, as I guessed, it is a Jesuit
expression. Paul has two advanced teaching degrees from Jesuit
Canisius College. For the good of the Order, he decided to talk
indoors about the history of New Ireland. And if there were any of
us left at the end, he would lead us up onto the mountain, passed
Thunder Rock, for a look at the storied ruins themselves.

He and his students have yarn after yarn about the place.
They have pictures and family histories and stories that are a
microcosm of the Irish Diaspora. He started in on the telling of it
and, being a descendant of that massive expatriation myself, I was
fascinated. I ate up every word. Though in his loquacious Irish
way, he did carry on and on. I began to think that he was
stretching a point here and there. Instead of raising an eyebrow at
the front of the room, I drifted to the back for a cup of coffee. I
thought it might enhance my attention span.

There I made the most marvelous discovery, chocolate Irish
potato cake made by our surely-to-be-sainted refreshment

chairman Lou Budnick. His cake was very moist and darkly delicious. The flavor of cinnamon broke through the chocolate and rang bells for me. I had to devour a second piece before I could summon the nerve to break into Paul's revelations and inform the group of my very own discovery. This proved difficult but finally Paul did close his mug for a well deserved breath of air. I stepped into the breach, pointed at the refreshment table and announced, "You are missing a miracle of a cake. It's made of rare oriental spices and rarer still 'chocolate Irish potatoes'."

Twelve of us apostles outlasted the talk and after eating our fill, we rendezvoused with Paul at the mountain-top parking lot within view of the great, calcified chunks of paleo-ocean bottom that are collectively called Thunder Rock. The sunny sky and warm, moist air were delicious to us as we milled about expectantly, then, one after another started swatting as a horde of tiny black flies engulfed us. I zoomed back to my car, hopped inside where I put on full bug gear including impervious parka, mittens and bug-net hat. They teased me a bit but by the time we finished the hike they were bidding over $100 for the hat alone.

New Ireland in Bug Season

It was warm inside all my layers of protection, as we climbed up and down grades, over old roads and along the grass-covered pipeline that conveys natural gas to and from sandstone storage in the dome under the center of the Park. But I did not begrudge the sweat, as others spit out bugs, wiped them from exposed skin and hooded them with whatever they had. There were muddy spots and puddles to splash through, too. Paul seemed immune to bugs, mud and exertion. He continued to unfold his torrent of information. He'd stop for a moment, or as long as the others could stand the insect attack, and jab a finger at a map. He'd be saying, "This end of the road wasn't used at the time. They came in the other end of it, from Limestone. There's no bridge across Irish Brook now and the beavers have built a dam so you can't come in that way." Or "OK, now where do you think the barn was?" or "Who can find the first foundation?"

He was talking every step of the way. Sometimes I'd be close enough to hear and sometimes not. In recollection, it is hard to distinguish when I heard or read what. He and his students first explored New Ireland in 1984. They have seen considerable deterioration in it since then. Old stone cellar walls have fallen in. Trees have fallen across foundations. Vegetation has grown up and many of the rusted-out buckets, tools and whiskey and milk bottles that were lying about have been carried off.

Paul said, "The rumor about New Ireland had been that in 1825, when the work on the Erie Canal was finished, Irish laborers were looking for a place like home to settle in. Some of them came to Limestone, NY and up on the mountain they built New Ireland." The kids from Paul's class found otherwise. There were twelve students like the twelve of us, and twelve New Ireland families. Each student took a family and developed all the information he could about that family. They checked census records, the county clerk's office and the tombstones in Saint Patrick's Catholic Cemetery in Limestone. They wrote to survivors and their children. They found old letters and they got in touch with Ennistymon, the small town in County Clare which these folks had left behind.

In the 1850's, following the great famine, times were still very poor in Ireland. John Carmody moved from Ennistymon to England where he married another Irish émigré, Mary O'Day.

They moved to New York where John got a job on a railroad running from New York to Pittsburgh by way of Limestone. They saved some money and in 1866, long after the completion of the Erie Canal, they bought 50 acres up on Irish Brook, west of Limestone. Their farm prospered. Gradually they expanded their holdings. Other neighbors and family from Ennistymon were so impressed with their stories of meat and milk on the table, of land and jobs that they clamored to come out here as well. The Carmodys helped them and the newcomers helped others till there were twelve farm homes in the colony.

The Carmodys, like the rest of them, had a big family, seven children. Even more hands than that were needed. Boys sent down from Father Baker's orphanage in Lackawanna were welcomed and found homes and work on the farms of New Ireland. But the big economic story was not farming. It was the discovery of oil. New Ireland sprung up just in time to catch the oil boom. The Carmody place, the most fortunate, had nine wells.

By the 1920s when Allegany State Park was being formed, the original inhabitants of New Ireland with their oil money and the skills they acquired in the oil industry had moved on. The place was deserted. Houses stood for a time. In the 1930's the Depression drove homeless people to squat there. After that, some of the wood and fittings are said to have been salvaged. The rest rotted away, leaving only moss-covered stone foundations that are gradually being taken over by the forest.

I had hiked in to New Ireland twice on my own. It is simple to get to the general vicinity of the ruins but if you are there after leaf-out, it can be a trick to actually locate them. When the New Ireland farms were working, the forest had been cleared. The beech, ash and maple have had eighty years to restore themselves. Alone there among the stone works and twisted thorn apple trees of New Ireland I had an eerie feeling. I was on someone else's property, prying about their homes, looking at the things they had left, at all the work they had done. I was intruding and unsure of my welcome.

Paul tells of others with such odd feelings. A woman uses the bridle path that passes close by New Ireland; she tells that whenever she gets to a certain spot she is overcome with sadness. She has to dismount and she sits and cries. A hunter fell asleep sitting on a log there and woke suddenly to see a woman in old-fashioned dress disappear down the road.

Life was not always easy. Many died young and in childbirth. Their lives and deaths are recorded in Saint Patrick's graveyard. Poor 21-year old Catherine McCarthy died in New Ireland when a house fell on her. Some say it is Catherine who wanders there still.

Just a few years ago Charlie Sheets, one of those Father Baker's boys who grew up in New Ireland, drove across the country and came home here. He was in his eighties and came ostensibly to dig up a tin can full of coins that he buried in his youth. Paul thinks it wasn't the money he was after but his youth. Charlie found this vastly changed place; laid himself down by a broken wall, went to sleep and died. Park police discovered his abandoned car at Thunder Rock and mounted a massive hunt. They found him at home here in New Ireland for his eternal rest.

Our group was pretty cheerful despite the inconvenience of spring hiking in the Park. The fresh air and sunshine made up for it and the fact that trees and brush were just greening up and not fully leafed made the layout of New Ireland more obvious. We found the spring that flowed into the dammed up pond that was the water source. We found the shallow foundation of a barn. There were several foundations of houses, none very large, but one was larger than most and had a perfectly preserved front walk. We gathered around that basement. Two huge trees lay across it where they had fallen, collapsing a section of the carefully cut and fitted masonry.

Someone handed Paul an iron hatchet head they had found. Paul handed it on to Bob Schmid, the custodian of many historical relics, and said, "I'd rather see you have this than for it to just wander off. We used to find lots of things, old shoes put together with wooden pegs, stoves and buckets, but it's all disappearing. That's why we need to get this place listed on the National Register of Historic Places and get some protection for it." Bob handed the hatchet to me. I tossed it into a bush.

At the time of the famine, my own Irish ancestors came out to America from the old country, the "old sod" they called it. They found homes and a way of life on this continent. But here on this spot, here in New Ireland, we have a unique record of this migration. Here are recorded the efforts of a few dozen impoverished Irish folk who left their homes in Europe to suffer in the holds of starvation and illness-ridden ships. They took up land. They built homes and built lives, and they moved on. What they survived, what they accomplished, they wrote here in rock. Paul is right; we must see that their record is preserved.

<u>Directions to New Ireland</u>: New Ireland is located on the U.S. Geological Survey 7.5 minute Limestone Quadrangle. From Red House go south on Allegany State Park Highway 2. At its intersection with France Brook Road turn left and go up the hill. Cross Ridge Road at the top and start down the old gravel road that goes into Limestone. About a quarter of a mile down the hill a much older dirt road takes off to the left and if you follow that about a mile you are in downtown New Ireland. You won't know it without looking carefully to either side of the road for its remains.

Another way in is to turn left at Ridge Road continue over to Thunder Rock instead of going down the hill. There is an unmarked but frequently trod trail out the back of Thunder Rock that leads to the old town site but this route is better taken in the company of someone who knows it.

Directions for Lou Budnick's Irish Chocolate Potato Cake:

1 cup butter	2 cups flour
2 cups sugar	1 tspn. baking powder
4 eggs	½ tspn. baking soda
3 ounces unsweetened	¼ tspn. salt
chocolate, melted	1 tspn. cinnamon
1 cup cold mashed potatoes	¼ tspn. nutmeg
¾ to 1 cup buttermilk	

Combine the ingredients in order given. Put into a greased, 9x13 baking pan and bake in a 350" oven for 35 minutes, or until done. Cool in pan for 10 minutes, then turn out and cool on a rack. Fill and ice with chocolate butter icing. Because this cake is very moist and will keep beautifully it needs a good, rich icing that will keep well and not dry out.

Rich Chocolate Butter icing

¼ cup butter
2 squares unsweetened chocolate, melted
3 cups icing sugar (at least)
Hot water to make the right consistency

Beat vigorously, add 1 teaspoon vanilla

Allegany, Yes
Cokeagany, No

John Arnold surprised our community by writing a letter to the News announcing and opposing a corporation taking over the Allegany State Park group camp known as Camp Allegany. By doing so it would displace the Buffalo Museum of Science there. John resents the take over because his kids have had such good experiences at Camp Allegany with the Museum. The Museum has been associated with the Park since 1924. It ran the world famous "School in the Forest" there in the thirties. It continues to run winter and summer programs in the Park.

Buffalo Museum Professors in Allegany in the 1930's

I did some investigating and wrote my own letter to the News:

Coca-Cola Co. wants to take over an Allegany State Park group camp. There are problems with this plan.

The State and Coca Cola have conducted these negotiations in the dark without opportunity for public comment.
In the past, Western New Yorkers have opposed the ceding over of parkland like Beaver Island, Joe Davis, and Fort Niagara for private use.

Allegany is threatened by private ownership of oil rights. Threats to log its forests have drawn massive protest.

The Buffalo Museum of Science and Cattaraugus County already have summer camps up and running at Camp Allegany, both of which serve inner city youth. Coca Coal would displace them. Camp Allegany is peculiarly well suited to the Buffalo Museum because it has family sized rooms that work well with Museum family weekend programs.

Coca Cola's proposed swimming pool would occupy a meadow. There is limited meadow habitat in the Park and this one is used for study. A pool is unnecessary with Red House Lake so near. The pool and its hazards would increase liability risk.

As for the proposed stable, there are already many horsemen using the park and their horses are hard on it. Sometimes they spoil sensitive places like Thunder Rock for foot traffic. The stable is not needed.

The Museum has been running year round programs with plans to expand them at Camp Allegany but the State's two year procrastination in signing a contract has been a road block. Without full management powers designated to one organization the various groups using the place have taken a toll.

To allow a corporation to use public property for advertising is bad precedent. Advertising is Coca Cola's bottom line motive. It is strikingly bad precedent that the product advertised is one to make our children fat and ruin their teeth.

If they have to eat sugar I'd prefer them in the Museum's Maple sugaring program.

Buffalo Museum Maple Sugaring

Finally, if the Park is forced to give into bribery, why not let Coke rehabilitate one of the older camps that are truly in need, Group Camp 10 or 12?

Why give away Camp Allegany, the site of summer camps with demonstrated effectiveness, the centerpiece of Allegany Group Camps? Keep our Buffalo Museum in Camp Allegany. Let Coke go ruin some one else's park.

Coca Cola Almost Buys
Camp Allegany
2002

Coca Cola, you taste so grand. You sparkle as I drink in your fresh cleansing sweetness. Empress of beverages, I love you. And you treat me so bad, faithless one. How you have rotted my teeth. You've made my kids so fat. Phosphorus flees from my bones before you. Wanton seducer, Coke, thy true name be osteoporosis.

And I love thee still. For me your companionship has so enhanced the most favorite of my foods. Without you what is a potato chip? But in thy company a chip is divinity. You slattern, oh faithless courtesan.

When my youth had fled you reinvented our union as Coke. In your presence my world grew young again. I am one with a new generation. With passion we pursue your charms. Yes, I want to give the world a song, a perfect melody. Things go better with Coca Cola. Things go better with Coke. Yes they do. They do. But look at the cost.

Hang the cost. Hit me again. Pop! Glug, glug, glug! Eeehmmm! Bur---rhp!

The hint that you and I are toying with cocaine sets our conjoined lips on fire. What a touch of harmless, evil, daring. Whether truth or lie, who cares? Score me that caffeine. Send my blood sugar on a lightning-streak. I am Coca Cola Man. Watch me rocket on high. Corporate America, watch me fly. I am your ideal.

Psst. Sonny boy, try a Coke, on the house. It'll put hair on your chest... or take it off. Tell the Principal you won't eat lunch unless there's Coke in the Cafeteria.

Mister Principal, let those kids have some fun, for Pete's sakes. Don't be a killjoy, health freako. Just give me exclusive pouring rights and I'll build you the new gym. Hell, I'll build two and I'll be yours to love forever.

Mr. Park Commissioner. Can't get a few lousy bucks out of the Governor? Want to fix those tumble-down shanty cabins? Sign right here. All I want is the 10 best weeks of the summer in that sweet little green beauty of a camp. Just going to run a little promotion there for the loveliest moneymaking seducer in the world. You can have the sweet thing back after we paint her Red, make her waters bubble and change her name to Coca Cola.

Red alert! Red alert! This is not a practice drill. This is an urgent emergency announcement.

The Coca Cola Company has offered the State of New York a very large but undisclosed sum of money for the summer use of the very best of group camps in Allegany State Park. This camp, presently known as Camp Allegany, is used by well-established agencies with long track records in the running of summer camps at that site. Those operations will be ousted. During the summer, Camp Allegany will be known as Camp Coca Cola.

Don't let your Park be stolen. Call Governor Pataki. Call Commissioner of Parks Castro. Picket the Governor's mansion. Arm the bears. Tell the deer to hide. Spread the word to the rabid raccoons. Mobilize.

For "Something evil this way comes" and be it Coca Cola or Coke, by any name its kiss is deadly sweet.

"And leave my meadow be."

FOX AND ME
A Kodiak Island Parable for Allegany

That early morning, Fox must have been watching from the shadows just out of sight.

The damp air reeked invitingly of fish and salt and seaweed. The first hint of a low-angled sun glistened off tiny wavelets on the bay.

In the shack, even our Inuit guide hadn't stirred yet. I was pleased to be up alone but a little worried about the creaking dock that led out into the bay. I tested the weathered boards with my weight. They held.

Around the dock's mossy pilings the water rustled persistently. That motion gave the only indication of the great bulging salmon that I knew were collected there. Those fish were preparing their final primordial run up the creek that slipped silently into the bay there. The waters of the creek had come down for the fish from jagged peaks at the center of the island, through the pine woods and tall grass. They finally merged with salt water here at the faded-red, tumbled-down ruin of a has-been fish cannery, turned has-been bear-hunting camp.

I stared at this moiling where the waters joined. I'm sure Fox did, too, as he watched my watching. Perhaps he felt bolder because I had grown still, fascinated at the sight of the watery commotion that we both knew meant fish. Maybe he mistook me for his friend, the bear-hunter guide, who worked here after the fisheries died.

I had learned of the relationship between those two the night before. As I prepared to crawl into my sleeping bag and just as the generator stopped and strangled the one bare light bulb, I noticed a sign above the chipped kitchen sink. Scrawled on white cardboard the over-wintering guide-caretaker had posted a warning to clients, "Do not discharge firearms within 200 yards of buildings. I have promised my friends they will not be shot."

There on the shore, did Fox suppose that I was his friend?

Fox took a cautious step from cover and abruptly placed himself in a corner of my vision. His russet body, ears at alert, nostrils wide, and one dark forepaw poised, registered and I reacted with a start. So did Fox. His startle landed him deep in the weeds beside the outhouse.

I froze. In a moment his pointed black snout and whiskered muzzle parted a patch of timothy. A pair of intelligent, wary, supplicant eyes searched out my intention, then swept past me toward where breakfast churned.

I held my breath. I, too, knew the sweet taste of fresh-caught salmon. But this visual treat, the vision of the bear-guide's old friend searching for sustenance left me oblivious to my own hunger.

Fox stepped forward, one, two, three quickening steps; at the edge of the gravel beach ten feet below he paused, staring at me. Glancing away he licked his thin lips.

I grinned a silent, go for it Fox. His head twitched toward me. His body tensed. That bit of movement in my face seemed to have poured adrenaline through him like a fire alarm. I froze.

Fox lowered his head, took another two tentative steps, then charged into the shallow, now boiling, turmoil and snatched a fish.

I marveled at such easy exact proficiency.

Fox, head held high, turned shoreward, burdened with this flopping, iridescent meal, half his own length, as it hung from either side of his refined jaw. He moved more slowly now but with great purpose.

As he stepped out of the wavelets on to the gravel he and I both heard the slip and clack of a lever action .38 caliber rifle. I jerked around. Fox jerked, too. In that moment of my incomprehension and his unwillingness to drop his catch, the rifle cracked.

"Grab that fish," my buddy whooped. "We got breakfast."

A feeling hit me in the gut just like that when coming into Red House over the hill from Salamanca I saw that pile of logs by the side of ASP 1. That great slash through the forest has been abandoned and is slowly recovering and maybe that Kodiak Fox with the quick reflexes escaped into the bush.

238

The Hellbender's tale has a ways to play out yet. Here's hoping that in the end it will tell of Allegany's return to the primeval forest where Gonusquah the stone giant and Gogansah, the false-face maker would be at home and where again the Hellbender will thrive.

Iroquois Dancer at Salamanca Pow Wow

Epilogue

Allegany Hellbender Tales is full of stories about things that happened in Allegany State Park. It is about oil men, the Civilian Conservation Corps, one room schools, campers, skiers, hikers, bird watchers, bear watchers, deer hunters, girls and boys, an ancient fortress and ghosts. But a recurrent theme runs through it. That theme is how will Allegany's forest, best, be managed to sustain this beloved Park. Allegany State Park forest issues never seem to come to a clear conclusion.

So that these issues don't get lost in the dust bin of government obscurity   and turn up as unhappy consequences down the road, here is a brief recap of where they stand in 2003:

The Master Plan, which took years of work, remains on the shelf. The choices it offers seem too politically-charged for it to be confirmed. The most troublesome of these choices is whether Allegany's timber should be allowed to mature into a climax forest or be harvested? Governor Pataki promised there would be no commercial logging in the Park. Since his promise there has been none. But there is no formalization of that policy.

National Fuel Gas continues to operate its 9000-acre natural gas storage field in the heart of the Park. It has backed off, for the time, from the expansion of that field into the old growth hemlock of the Big Basin. It's pipelines criss-cross the Park. It continues to have an interest in buying mineral rights under the Park.

The mineral rights to half of the Park remain in private ownership and the State has made no progress toward purchasing them.

The proposed cutting up of the forest with roads to plug abandoned oil wells has not happened.

There are still too many and too poorly fed deer in the Park. They are eating out the understory of the forest impeding its regeneration.

The snowmobile trail through the Art Roscoe cross-country ski area stands incomplete and mostly unused.

There is a chronic shortfall of cash for the Park so that OPRHP is tempted to accept offers from companies like Coca Cola that amount to giving away chunks of the Park for advertising. Coke has withdrawn.

The Summit Fire Tower restoration funds are in place and the project is on track.

A citizen's advisory committee is helping the Park manage the trail system equitably with minimal disruption of the forest.

The Allegany State Park administration soldiers on maintaining this magnificent Park despite budget crunches, personnel shortages, competing users, and the demanding pressures of nature, politics and conscience. While balancing all these, they keep a smiling face toward the people visiting the Park and keep their doors open to those with opinions about the Park.